COURTING

SUCCESS

To my best friend Eileen,
you are like sunshine on
a rainy day — you make
everything more fun and you
are always there when I need
you most — I am so
blessed to have you in my
family.

Love
Me

COURTING

SUCCESS

MUFFET MCGRAW'S
Formula for Winning—
in Sports and in Life

Muffet McGraw with Paul Gullifor

TAYLOR TRADE PUBLISHING
Lanham • New York • Toronto • Oxford

Published by Taylor Trade Publishing
An imprint of The Rowman & Littlefield Publishing Group, Inc.
4501 Forbes Boulevard, Suite 200
Lanham, Maryland 20706

Distributed by National Book Network

Library of Congress Cataloging-in-Publication Data

McGraw, Muffet.
    Courting success : Muffet McGraw's formula for winning—
in sports and in life / Muffet McGraw with Paul Gullifor. —
1st Taylor Trade Pub. ed.
        p. cm.
    Includes bibliographical references and index.
    ISBN 1-58979-027-8 (hardcover : alk. paper)
    1. McGraw, Muffet. 2. Basketball coaches—United States—
Biography. 3. Women basketball coaches—United States—Biography.
4. University of Notre Dame—Basketball. 5. Lady Irish (Basketball
team) I. Gullifor, Paul F. II. Title.
GV884.M24 A3 2003
796.323'092—dc22   2003014228

⊗™ The paper used in this publication meets the minimum requirements
of American National Standard for Information Sciences—Permanence
of Paper for Printed Library Materials, ANSI/NISO Z39.48–1992.
Manufactured in the United States of America.

To Matt

My husband, my hero, my soul mate, and my best friend.

I knew from the first moment I saw you that I would love you forever.

To Murph

You are the reason I believe in miracles.

—MUFFET MCGRAW

This book is dedicated to women basketball players . . .

. . . the coaches who teach them . . .

. . . and the parents who love them.

—PAUL GULLIFOR

CONTENTS

FOREWORD

After a long and complicated drive through the dirt roads of Indiana, Coach McGraw finally found the house and offered a tall, unpolished country girl an opportunity to play basketball for the University of Notre Dame—for this I will be eternally grateful. The recruiting process can be confusing for a teenager who is being courted by numerous different universities, because each is accompanied by a unique set of promises for her future. There was something sincere and real to what Coach McGraw was offering: a great education and basketball success that was dependent on my level of dedication—all of this done with the emphasis of a "family-like" atmosphere. She not only fulfilled the promises she made that day, but exceeded far and beyond what I had imagined.

At first glance of the tiny frame pacing the sidelines, you may think Coach McGraw is an intense competitor with a fiery Irish spirit—all of which is correct. She has an endless passion for the sport of basketball and an amazing ability to transform immature high school players into talented college athletes. As good as she is at developing players, she is even better at converting them into 12 individuals who work effectively together to produce a successful team.

With a great deal of admiration, I watched how Coach managed to run an elite basketball program and never lose sight of her devotion to Matt and Murphy (husband and son). I have strong family values and was grateful to play for a coach who had the same. Her dedication was not limited to her immediate family—she strove to create the same atmosphere with her team. The basketball team truly became my home away from home.

There were three major factors that influenced my decision to accept the scholarship to Notre Dame—it is a top academic university, I would be playing for a good basketball program on the rise to greatness, and Coach McGraw. My four years at Notre Dame were indeed life shaping. From heartbreaking losses to the ultimate level of success, I learned how to handle pressure, what it takes to be a leader, and how to balance my faith, family, academics, and basketball. I will forever be grateful to Coach McGraw for giving me the opportunity to attend Notre Dame, for instructing me, guiding me, and pushing me to achieve my academic and athletic goals, and, most of all, for the continual support she shows in my life outside of Notre Dame.

—RUTH RILEY

PREFACE

I f you ask young men who their basketball heroes are, you'll get the usual answers: Michael, Shaq, LeBron. If you ask young women the same question, the response might be silence. There aren't many role models in the sports world available for young women athletes, and that fact inspired me to convince Coach Muffet McGraw to tell her story.

By any measure Coach McGraw is a success. The University of Notre Dame's football reputation is well known, but in the shadows of the nation's most storied football program, Muffet McGraw has quietly built the women's basketball program into a national power.

Arguably, women's basketball has been the university's most consistently successful varsity sport. Over the past 16 years, the Notre Dame women's basketball team has made 13 postseason appearances, including 10 trips to the NCAA tournament. The team's rise to national prominence was underscored with a national championship in 2001. In short, the Notre Dame women's basketball program has been steadily built into a perennial national championship contender, and its architect for those 16 years has been Head Coach Muffet McGraw.

Hired in May 1987, Muffet McGraw wasted little time in bringing national recognition to the women's basketball program. Fourteen of Coach McGraw's 16 teams at Notre Dame have won 20-plus games, including four straight in her first four seasons, and a current streak of 10 straight. She has more than 300 victories at Notre Dame and a winning percentage of .72. She has led Notre Dame to all 10 of the school's NCAA tournament appearances.

The numerous awards attest to Muffet McGraw's coaching success. In 2001 alone, she was named the Women's Basketball Coaches Association National Coach of the Year, the Naismith's Women's College Coach of the Year, and the Associated Press' Coach of the Year. Additionally, that season she was *Sports Illustrated for Women's* Coach of the Year and the Big East Conference Coach of the Year.

Personal accolades aside, Coach McGraw is more concerned with off-court success than the progress of her teams. Accordingly, this book, designed to motivate and inspire young athletes, is one in which Coach Muffet McGraw shares her formula for success—on and off the basketball court. The book provides valuable lessons for those aspiring toward success in basketball, and in life, while illustrating why Muffet McGraw is one of college basketball's most accomplished coaches and a wonderful role model for young women athletes.

ACKNOWLEDGMENTS

Thanks to Paul Gullifor for his patience and guidance, and for making this such a fun and memorable experience.

Thanks to all of my St. Joe teammates and coaches, especially Mary Maley, Kathy Langley, Chrissy McGoldrick, Mary Sue Garrity, and Ellen Ryan, for sharing my passion and love of the game.

To the T's for sharing their wisdom and experience, for giving me their shoulders to lean on, and for friendships I will treasure forever—Eileen Woods, Sally Derengoski, and Jan Halperin.

My sincere thanks to the best staff in college basketball: Carol Owens, Coquese Washington, Kevin McGuff, Letitia Bowen, Heather Clay, and Jeri Lucas.

Thanks to all of the players who contributed to building this program into a national champion. The process is described well by a quote from Jacob Riis.

When nothing seems to help, I go and look at the stonecutter hammering away at his rock perhaps a hundred times without as much as a crack showing in it. Yet at the hundred and first blow it will split in two, and I know it was not that blow that did it—but all that had gone before.

Thanks to Father Monk Malloy, Kevin White, and Sandy Barbour for their unwavering support.

Thanks also to my mom and dad for believing in me from my very first game as head coach. And to my sisters—Kathy Derr, Patti Mento, and Peg Schiavoni—for being there when I needed them most, and for their constant encouragement, support, loyalty, and love. And to my brothers—Joe, Michael, and Tom O'Brien—for showing me how tough I needed to be to compete in a man's world.

—MUFFET MCGRAW

Thanks to all who made this book possible, especially Muffet McGraw for trusting me to tell her story. I learned a lot about basketball from Coach McGraw. Thanks also to Matt McGraw, who was eager to share his memories of Notre Dame basketball. The McGraws were wonderful to work with, and we became good friends in the process.

A special thanks to Chris Masters in the Sports Information Department at the University of Notre Dame for his willingness and eagerness to help. I'd also like to thank all of the people connected with the Rowman & Littlefield Publishing Group, especially Jill Langford for her editing skills and Tracy Miracle for her marketing expertise. Thanks to all of the young athletes, particularly women basketball players whom I have coached through the years, for providing the inspiration for this book. The reason I wrote this book was to provide a role model for young women basketball players, and there is no better role model than Muffet McGraw.

Thanks to my family: my wife, Shelley, and my three children, Sarah, Daniel, and Ali, for the freedom to pursue this project, and the support to make it happen. Finally, thanks to all who supported me in this project whether through ideas and suggestions or simply with best wishes and encouragement.

—PAUL GULLIFOR

1 ACCEPTING ROLES

Everybody on a championship team doesn't
get publicity,
But everyone can say he or she was a champion.

—MAGIC JOHNSON

Whenever you're on a team, whether it is a sports team, a family, or work environment, you have a role to play. The most important message I have to communicate to players is that each of them has a role, and that role is based upon what each player does well. Not everyone can be the star, which is probably the hardest lesson for most of my players to learn, because they come from high school environments where they were stars. In many cases, the whole high school program was built around them, but having graduated to the college level, they find themselves almost immediately where they have to make some sacrifices to their personal goals. Chances are very good that they won't see their name in the newspapers as often as they did in high school, and it's not easy to go from being "the go-to player" to someone who fills a role. That high school star may not even get a lot of playing time in college. She might now become the person who comes off the bench. But her attitude, and how she accepts that role, will determine the team's success. That's true in basketball and it's true in life.

It's that way in the family. When you have a big family, everyone has different strengths and weaknesses, and roles are assigned by what those strengths are. I come from a big family. My mother was a traditional stay-home mom. She did the housework while my dad's role was that of the breadwinner. My brothers did all the outdoor chores. My sisters and I did all of the indoor chores (although at times I rebelled against these roles!). It's the parents' job to identify strengths and nurture them in their children, and, similarly, it's my job as a coach to make every player feel important.

If you come to Notre Dame as a really good 3-point shooter, we're going to have you shoot a lot of 3-pointers. If you're Ruth Riley, at six-foot-five inches, you won't be shooting 3-pointers. You're going to be down around the basket. Only one player can take the last shot, and you might not be the one to take an important shot, *but what you do is still important.* This is the biggest challenge to any coach—getting the players to buy into their roles. All any player really wants is to feel she is an important part of the program, and it's the coach's job to make players feel that they are contributing. We couldn't be successful without the twelfth "man," and I couldn't be successful without the support staff and assistant coaches. The fact is, nobody succeeds alone.

I have to admit, this was an adjustment for me as a coach. When I first started coaching, I had a starting five and paid very little attention to the substitutes. This is probably because, as a player, I always played. I was a starter and never sat the bench. In those early years, I never really understood how crucial it was to involve everyone, and make everyone feel important. I even used to avoid talking to some players who thought they deserved more playing time because I didn't want the confrontation. But over time I've learned that every player on the team can contribute, and it's the player who determines what her role is (with a little help from the coach, of course!). Your job might be to work as hard as possible in practice and make the person in front of you better. When you're on the bench in a game, your job is to be positive, to be a cheerleader, to be the first one up high-fiving a teammate. Your job might be simply to be as encouraging as possible.

The hard part of coaching is communicating this to players. There is a fine line. A player might think I've lost confidence in her if her role is diminished, while I'm thinking of what's best for the team. I have to constantly preach the team concept.

I've found this can be a personality issue, too. Last year, I gave our team the Myers-Briggs personality test at the end of the season, and I took it myself. Formally called the Myers-Briggs Type Indicator, it is one of the most widely used personality instruments in the world. It's a self-report test that increases self-understanding and appreciation of personal differences.

It's fascinating because I discovered that my personality is much different from most of my players, with the exception of Alicia Ratay, who, to my surprise, has the same personality as me. Alicia is introverted. She shies away from the limelight and really dislikes public speaking. Although Alicia is quiet, when she speaks she's very direct. She doesn't sugarcoat anything.

I don't care for the limelight either. Public speaking is not my favorite thing to do, but it's part of my job. Like Alicia, my personality tends to be direct. I deal with the facts, and I'm very straightforward. I'm a thinker, not a feeler. I make decisions based on facts, not emotion. What this means is I'll sometimes hurt a player's feelings without even knowing it. It was enlightening for the players to see the results of the test. They now know where I'm coming from. They expect me to be more emotional and caring. So when I tell a player she's shooting 12 percent from 3-point range and it's time for her to move in, what she hears is, "The coach doesn't have any confidence in me." As a coach, you have to know the players' personalities so you can know what they're hearing, because most of the time they're not hearing what you're saying. Coaches often get accused of being negative, when they're just realistic and honest. When players aren't realistic about their own abilities, and their parents aren't either, it can cause problems. It might be the first time in her young life that a coach has told her to STOP shooting.

Because the Myers-Briggs Test was so enlightening to my staff, my team, and me, I plan to do the test at the beginning of each year. I really believe it helps define roles, as well as the best way to communicate those roles to players. It can help identify the team leaders especially. Players' roles are assigned very early in the season. Two years ago we had six freshmen. In the beginning of the year I told them we were going to go through the first two weeks of practice, and that they could play however they wanted to play. They could shoot the shots that they wanted to shoot, and they could play like they wanted to play. At the end of those two weeks I sat them down and told them here's what you're good at, and here's what we need you to do. And it's really interesting to see that when everyone has the green light to do what she wants, basically players play to their strengths. I do this every year now. We keep statistics, and at the end of that two-week period I go around the room in front of the whole team and point out the shooters from the nonshooters, the rebounders from the ball-handlers. I need to be honest with them, and tell them here's how it will be. It's good to do this in front of the team so that everyone knows everyone else's role. Often times the crowd, and very often the parents, can be yelling at a player to shoot it, but that may not be her role, and all her teammates know it. If a player doesn't like her role, it's probably because it doesn't involve her scoring. But show me a player unwilling to accept her role, and I'll show you a selfish player.

Selfish players will keep you from being successful. You don't ever really know if a player is selfish or not until you get her here on campus because all the high school coaches say the same thing about their players: "Best kid I've ever coached, hardest worker I've ever had, so coachable," etc. Well, yeah, that may be true because the coach never had to yell at her, and never took her out of a game. So when she comes here, not only is she getting yelled at, but also she's sitting on the bench and not playing much. That's a huge adjustment for a player because the biggest issue with women, by far, is their confidence. Every player goes through a point where she has totally lost her confidence. It doesn't matter how good she is. They all go through it.

It's great to have a recruit who plays for a high school coach who challenges her, because you can see how she handles it. When she comes out of a game, you get to see if she is cheering for her teammates, focusing on the game, and listening to the coach. I also look carefully at a recruit's relationship with her parents. We have had recruits where you go into her home for the home visit, and the home is a shrine to the child. There are trophies and awards everywhere. This might indicate a selfish player. That makes me want to walk right out the back door. It is the biggest turnoff, because the parents are living through their daughter. The best players I've had were just the opposite. The classic example is Beth Morgan, who played for us from 1993 to 1997. When I went to her house on a recruiting visit I asked her, "Where are all the trophies?" She said, "I don't know, probably in the attic boxed up somewhere." I could just tell, here is someone who has her priorities in order. But then her father is a coach so you knew she would be a joy to coach.

There's a difference when an athlete can tell you she averages "19.3 points per game" versus the one who says, "I don't know, maybe 15 or so." In other words, you can tell the ones who are high on their own statistics. We also talk to them about their coaches, and you'd be amazed how many complain about their coaches. They'll complain about their coach's philosophy or the coach's lack of basketball knowledge. That's when I say goodbye (I have this solidarity with coaches that, no matter what, I'm on the coaches' side).

The relationship they have with their parents is the kind of relationship I'm going to have with them. So if a young lady is respectful and thankful and appreciative of her parents, she's going to be that way here with me. That's the kind of player I want, not the one who demands the credit card and heads for the bookstore when she visits Notre Dame. All of these things, though seemingly minor, could be signs of a selfish player, and selfish players won't accept roles.

The other thing we do when we bring recruits on campus is have them spend a lot of time with the team. Then we ask every player on the team what she thought of the recruit. Is she going to fit in or not? We've probably only had a few prospects in the past 15 years where the team was genuinely concerned about her fitting in. In that case, we drop the prospect from further consideration. That may seem like a lot of input to give a team, but the team's evaluation is critical, and I've actually put more emphasis on this evaluation through the years. In the earlier years I used to be more likely to say to the team, "Like her or not, she's a great athlete and we need her." But that's not true anymore. The team's evaluation is extremely important to me.

When we first started recruiting, we felt we had to get the best players, and so we'd promise them anything. But now team chemistry is our number one priority, and we don't promise them anything except a great education. Chemistry is just a euphemism for players who accept roles. Good players want to play with good players, and they expect that they will earn their playing time. They know coming in that nothing will be handed to them, and they have to work for it. When you first start to build a program, you have to sell the prospects and constantly build them up. You have to build them up so much that when they get to school, they have to fail because they can't possibly be as good as you made them out to be. I want kids who come on campus and are blown away by Notre Dame. When they go to a football game, and the band is playing, there are 80,000 fans, and the sun is shining, I want them to be excited. I would rather take a kid who really wants to be here, even though she may not be in the top 30 or 40 in America. I'll take a good player who really wants to be here any day over a top-10 athlete I had to convince to come here. She's going to be happy, so she'll be successful, and so will the team. I don't try to talk kids into something they don't want.

A player who refuses to accept her role will be unhappy, and usually ends up transferring. I also tell them that if they don't like their role, then they should use the summer to change it. Everybody wants to be a 3-point shooter. So use the summer to shoot 3-pointers, then come back in the fall and prove to me that you can fill that role. But what about the good defender, or the person who can drive well to the hoop? We need those folks, too. When Katy Flecky was a freshman, she thought she could expand her game from the post to the perimeter. Everyone else, I think, was okay with her role. I told Katy we needed her around the basket, but she wanted to come outside and shoot threes. Interestingly enough, she won me over. I don't think she ever shot a three during her freshman season, but she did during our exhibition trip to Italy after that season. She wanted to make that adjustment. She worked on her game, and during practice she jumped into the guard spots. She did well enough that the coaches agreed that she could probably do that for us. *You should play to your strengths but keep working on your weaknesses.*

On our national championship team, we had two players who really epitomized role acceptance, and it's not the players most people think of. I'm referring to Imani Dunbar and Meaghan Leahy. Imani was a backup point guard who never really got a lot of playing time. She grew into the role of being the backup. By "growing into it," I mean her role acceptance came with maturity. This was more difficult to teach when they first arrived, but as seniors they understood. Imani and Meaghan became cheerleaders, they were encouraging, and they worked hard in practice. There is no doubt they had as much to do with our national championship as anything that Ruth Riley or Niele Ivey did on the floor. In fact, they were happy for Ruth and Niele, and they were happy for themselves because they got a national championship ring. They learned that being a small part of something big is just as good as being the star.

Of course, our starters on that team also had to accept their roles, and they did. The year before the national championship we had terrible chemistry, and terrible role acceptance. We had two players in particular who really didn't want to accept their roles. A year later, once they accepted their roles, we became a very good team.

Ruth Riley was our "go-to player." That was her role. When we needed a basket she was going to get it. Her job was to score and rebound. She could never take a night off. She was not allowed to get into foul trouble. Ruth was a great leader. And she never took a day off, either. In fact, I couldn't get her to take a day off. When I'd give the team a day off, Ruth would be here shooting, or she'd be in the weight room. We actually worried that she was going to wear herself out.

Sometimes we'd call time-out in a game just to say Ruth wasn't getting the ball often enough. We used to talk about her touching the ball at least every other possession. We keep track of every single possession so we knew how often she was getting it. That team took three years to get to the point where everyone accepted her role.

Alicia Ratay's role was to be on the same side as Ruth so they couldn't double down on Ruth. Alicia was a great shooter, and opposing defenses couldn't leave her alone. They had to defend her. Her job was to shoot, especially threes. You can't tell someone to *make* shots, but you can sure tell her to *take* them. If she didn't shoot, I'd take her out and tell her again that we needed her to shoot. It probably looks to the fan like she did nothing wrong, but not shooting when you're a shooter is wrong because it's not good for the team. You are not filling your role. This is harder to do if you don't have a strong bench, but we were fortunate to have some good shooters on the bench. In one sense this took the burden off of Alicia to score, but she also knew she could be replaced if she didn't shoot. I wanted Alicia on the floor because even when she wasn't shooting, other teams still had to guard her. For coaches, all we have is playing time to modify behavior. We can't control *how* the team plays, but we *can* control *who* plays, and *how much she plays*.

It's *everyone's* role to play defense and rebound. Everyone rebounds on both ends of the court. Our team goal is to lead the nation in all defensive statistics. That championship season we led the nation in field goal percentage defense, and we were in the top five teams in points allowed.

Niele Ivey's role was to run the team and get the ball to the right people, mainly Ruth. She had the green light to shoot if she was open. A good passer, Niele could also drive. The point guard has the most crucial role on any team. I tell point guards straight up that I will be hardest on them, and that they may even cry a bit during their freshman year. I think most of what goes wrong on the floor is the point guard's fault. A point guard's role is to get the ball to people when they are open and can do something with it. If someone receives a pass, but can't do anything with it, and she ends up traveling, that's the point guard's fault. Niele was a great free throw shooter, and great at stealing the ball, but her job primarily was to run the team. She had to learn to think and direct the team at the same time, and she was the best in the nation by her senior year.

Kelley Siemon's role was to help keep the double team away from Ruth and run the floor for the fast break. Defensively, she was to give up her body for the team, take the charge, and keep Ruth out of foul trouble. She was so unselfish and, yet, Kelly Siemon had a really bad junior year. I took her out of the starting lineup that season because she wasn't playing well. She came into her senior year with a better understanding of what she needed to do to fill her role. Kelley is a great example of someone who accepted her role for the good of the team. She probably could have done more had she gone to another school. The linebacker's daughter, she was one tough, tough kid. She played in the UConn game that season with a broken hand. We substituted for her often in the end of that game to try to keep her off the foul line. She accepted that because she knew she was not a good free throw shooter, especially with the broken hand! She knew what was best for the team. That was a team that accepted roles because those players wanted to win.

Kelley also filled the role of comic relief. She memorized movie lines and could practically recite them on cue. During especially tense times, she could retrieve a line from *What about Bob* or some other movie and instantly deflate the pressure.

Erica Haney was known as "the athlete." She defended well. She rebounded well. She was the one that other teams forgot to defend. They had to concentrate on Ruth but also pay attention to Niele and Alicia.

While I'll discuss roles with my players, I try not to discuss roles with their parents. If parents want to talk about issues involving their daughter, I have no problem with that. Sometimes you get a different perspective of what's going on when you keep the communication lines open with parents. I've learned that players who have a good relationship with their parents will tell them things

they don't tell the coach, and if the coach has a good relationship with the parents, it can really help. I would rec-
ommend as a coach that you try to keep the lines of
communication open with the parents.

Of course certain positions have to be filled by the
players. Years ago, these were simply called guards, for-
wards, and centers. The terminology has changed, and we
tend to number these positions today.

For example, the "one" refers to the point guard. The
"one" has to have a great mental game in terms of her ability to understand offenses. She has to be able to handle the
ball and see the floor. The "one" has to be a great decision
maker. She has to know who our scorers are and get them
the ball. We expect her to be a coach on the floor, and so
we are pretty hard on our point guards, and so they have
to have tough skins. I'm very selective in recruiting "ones."
I want point guards who *can* score but don't necessarily
have to score, because they need to be unselfish with the
ball. I also like "ones" who are emotional, because I need
them to motivate and inspire their teammates. Niele Ivey
and Coquese Washington are two of the better "ones"
we've had at Notre Dame. Another great point guard was
Mary Gavin. I only had the pleasure of coaching her for
her senior year, but she is our all-time assist leader.

The "two" guard needs to be a good shooter. I want
somebody who can shoot the three. She also has to be a
good ball handler because she's expected to help bring the
ball up the court against pressure. Speed is more important for the "one," while you can get away with slower feet
at the "two." It's good if the "two" can also put the ball on
the floor and take it to the hole. She should be a little more

physical than the "one." In a lot of programs, including ours, there is a trend to go without a true "two" and basically have two point guards. Sheila McMillan was one of the best "twos" I've ever coached.

The "three," sometimes referred to as a "shooting forward" or "small forward," is usually the most talented player on the team. This player is a jack-of-all-trades. We like "threes" to be at least six feet tall. She has to be able to post up inside and shoot the three outside. She has to be able to handle the ball and make entry passes inside. This player has to have a perimeter game *and* an inside game. She has to be a great rebounder, too. Most successful teams have a really good player at this position. Beth Morgan, our all-time leading scorer, was a "three," as was Alicia Ratay. Jackie Batteast currently fills this position.

The "four," or power forward, has to be able to post up. It's a bonus if she can step outside and knock down a shot, but primarily she is a post-up player. In some of our offenses, the "four" and "five" are basically interchangeable. In some offenses, if we don't have a true "five," the "three" and "four" are interchangeable. The "four" has to enjoy playing physical. She has to be an aggressive rebounder. Kelley Siemon was a great "four" for Notre Dame.

The "five," or center, camps around the basket. She needs to post players up and rebound. It's a huge advantage if the "five" can also run. A "five" who can get up and down the floor is a great bonus. Ruth Riley, Katryna Gaither, and Teresa Borton are examples of excellent "fives."

In 2001, I recruited a class of six players. Of course, only five can play, and none of them were true "ones" (point guards). Role acceptance was a huge challenge there. But if you look at other successful programs, they'll rotate seven or eight players. We can do that. It doesn't matter who starts. Who starts a game is not nearly as important as who finishes.

I don't use my full allotment of scholarships because that is just too many people to keep happy. The first year we went to the Final Four we had eight players because of injuries. I think 11 is good, but I can deal with 10. It used to be we needed 10 for practice, but now we scrimmage against men quite a bit. Most teams only play about eight people in a game anyway, sometimes seven. Sometimes fewer. Our championship team played with only six. We couldn't really press, and we couldn't foul much, so we played zone. One coach told me no team has ever won a national championship playing a 2-3 zone. I'm happy to say we proved her wrong.

Sometimes roles have to be adjusted during the season, and a good coach has to be willing and flexible enough to make those adjustments. It can be evolutionary. We transformed into a team where Jacqueline Batteast is going to be our scorer. That's her role. When she went down with an injury two years ago, Alicia Ratay averaged 26 points per game. Alicia really stepped up, which was hard for her because she didn't want to shoot that much. Somebody else who stepped up was Katy Flecky, who became a starter. We told the team, "We've just lost 15 points and 10 rebounds per game in Jackie. One person doesn't have to replace that. But if everyone on the team picks up two more points and one more rebound, we'll be fine."

Alicia Ratay was unselfish, to a fault. Yet, if we were down three and needed a shot, she was ready. What is interesting about Alicia is she didn't mind taking the big shot; she just didn't want to take a lot of them during a game. And you're talking about someone who was highly efficient as a shooter. She led the nation in shooting percentage three years ago. She holds the NCAA record for three-point shooting percentage in a four-year period. So, I was constantly saying, "shoot it!" She just didn't like to miss! We used to talk to her before each season, and she thought it was a joke. I would tell her to take more shots, and she would just say, "Okay." I once asked her, "How many shots do you think you could take in a game?" And she said, "How many do you want me to take?" I replied, "Let me put it this way, how many shots do you think you can miss?" She said, "Not many." Alicia wasn't one to go 4 for 17. She'd go 4 for 10 instead.

Sometimes during the course of a season, one player's role will increase. Of course, that means someone else's role will diminish. From my experience, the player with the diminished role will most often take that out on the coach, rather than display jealousy toward the player with the more prominent role. The player with the diminished role will usually believe that I've lost confidence in her. This often spirals downward. She believes I've lost confidence in her, so she begins playing like it. Here's the challenge in coaching: how do you get players to understand that what you're doing is for the benefit of the team? It's up to the player to start playing better. It's not my responsibility to keep a player in the game until she starts playing better.

One role that has to be filled is the leadership role. You can't win without a team leader. This is the single most important ingredient in winning. Look at every national champion and you'll find a great leader on that team. Our national championship team had a triumvirate of leadership: Ruth, Kelley, and Niele. I prefer the leader to be a point guard because she has the ball and is naturally in position to command others.

This whole lesson in role acceptance probably comes from being a former point guard myself. I was not allowed to shoot. That was not my job. I played with an All-American shooter, and my job was to get her the ball and to be a defensive stopper. I was fine with that, because I wanted to win. I really didn't care if I scored a point, as long as we won. Now when I tell a player not to shoot because she's not a good shooter, she looks at me like I'm crazy. I expect her to accept that, because I want to win. That's all that matters.

Other coaches no doubt formed some of my beliefs. I was only an assistant for two years, but I learned a lot from my mentor, Jim Foster. I wish I could have been an assistant longer, for different people. I think it would be great to have a sabbatical, where I could go spend one week with every coach in America. You get used to your own way of doing things. I like to hire assistants because they bring new ideas, and you can learn a lot from wherever they just came.

One area of role acceptance that is rarely addressed is in the coaching staff. Coaches and assistant coaches also have to accept roles. When Kevin McGuff came here, Carol Owens had only been here one year. Both coaches were very young and just starting out. I gradually gave them more and more responsibility as they earned it. I think that approach works better than bringing them in and assigning their roles from the start. Just like I do with my players, I like to put coaches in situations where they're going to be successful, for the good of the team. It was the same with Coquese Washington. When she came in, she coached the guards, but she has expanded her role into other areas of the offense.

I once hired a former head coach as an assistant and learned that that's a difficult transition to make. This coach was used to being in charge and had trouble accepting the new role as an assistant. It led to conflicts and was ultimately counterproductive. It is much easier to go from assistant coach to head coach rather than vice versa. I don't necessarily think you have to be a really good assistant to be a good head coach. I was a horrible assistant coach. I like to make the decisions. I think every assistant coach gets to that point where he or she wants to be the decision maker. I can see this in my assistants. It's easy to tell when an assistant is ready to become a head coach, and most assistants want their own program eventually. And that's good. I want assistant coaches with that kind of aspiration and ambition. Otherwise, they're content where they are, and contentment often invites complacency.

Actually, it is my job to help them get that head coaching job. I have as much responsibility to these coaches as I do to my players. Kevin McGuff took the job at Xavier and I'm happy for him. It's a good job, a good fit, and he's ready for it. I have to be as honest with coaches as I am with players, which means if I don't think an assistant coach is ready for a head coaching job, I tell him or her.

I have to admit, though, I don't like playing against former assistant coaches. I don't want to play Xavier. I told

Kevin not to tell the Xavier people you can schedule Notre Dame, because I'm not playing Xavier! I consider that when scheduling and purposefully avoid playing teams coached by former assistants. I'm just too competitive, and these people are my friends.

I expect the coaches to provide a unified front. We may have our disagreements privately, and we do, but in front of the team we must be totally in sync philosophically, and I expect that kind of loyalty from my assistants. Disagreements are good, even healthy for a team, but there is a point where everyone must accept the decision for the good of the team.

My assistants are usually very young and, as a result, most of them arrive here very inexperienced at coaching, but I've discovered that coaching experience is only one thing to look at when making hiring decisions. For example, when Carol arrived, I knew I was getting someone who was one great low post player, and I really needed someone who could coach post players. The second thing I liked about Carol was her ability to recruit. When I met her, I instantly liked and respected her. I thought that high school players and their parents were going to love her. She makes a great impression. It worked. She has upgraded our recruiting significantly.

When I interviewed Kevin, I gave him a basketball. I told him I was a guard, so I asked him to show what he can teach me. He lit up and showed me drill after drill. He played in college, which I think is a big plus, and I was sold. That was an easy hire. Youth on the coaching staff is an advantage, especially in relating to young players on the recruiting trail. I have nothing in common with

17-year-olds, but my assistants can relate to them much better than I can.

I do have a little trouble hiring a former player to coach with me. I'd prefer they get out and get some experience for a couple of years elsewhere first. That way they'll come here with some new philosophies and ideas.

By the way, just because one was a great player doesn't mean one can be a great coach. Sometimes great players never had to learn a lot about technique. They were so gifted athletically that they got by without absorbing the fundamentals. Consequently, when they have to teach a player who is not so athletic, they struggle.

I've learned a lot from the men's basketball coaches who have been at Notre Dame: Digger Phelps, Fran McCaffery, and now Mike Brey. I watch the men's practices here, and not just the Notre Dame men. When Syracuse came here to play, I went to watch them. They run the same 2-3 zone defense that we use, and Jim Boeheim showed me all of the traps and so forth. It was like having my own private clinic. I talk to Mike Brey and his assistants often. It doesn't matter if it's men or women. Basketball is basketball.

What you learn on the basketball court can teach you lessons for life. This probably sounds cliché, but basketball really is a microcosm of life. You will face a lot of adversity in life, and learning how to handle adversity in sports will help you handle the bumps in the road in your life. You will have to accept roles, the role in your family and the role in your career. The Xs and Os are about 10 percent of my job. The rest of it is managing people. I want them to grow. I want them to learn. The fun part is seeing them come in as wide-eyed freshmen and seeing them leave as mature, responsible, and disciplined young women. It is such a joy to watch the women I've coached playing in the WNBA. I'm really proud of them. I feel like their mom when I'm watching them play.

Teaching life lessons is another thing I've learned. When I first started coaching, I was a dictator. It was *my* way or the highway, don't ask me or tell me, because you don't have an opinion. You have *my* opinion. I never used to teach a lot of "life lessons." I was only focused on winning. It was only recently, maybe within the past five years, that I've really felt like there is more to life than basketball. Basketball is important only if it teaches about life, and role acceptance is a huge part of life.

② ACCOUNTABILITY

Don't tell me how rocky the sea is,
Just bring the darned ship in!

—LOU HOLTZ

Accountability is another one of life's lessons that all players need to learn. We teach this in every area of our players' college life. We don't have a lot of rules in terms of our players' behavior off the court. We simply tell them, "Don't do anything that will embarrass you or the program." When you are part of this program, you are on a pedestal. When you go into the community, people know you, so you have to be very careful how you act, how you dress, and how you treat people.

I tell my players that their behavior and personal presentation reflect not just on them but also on the program, the university, and me. If a player wears sweats to class, sits in the back, and falls asleep, that professor is going to say, "That women's basketball team doesn't care about academics." Even if you're the only player that professor has taught, that will be his or her opinion of the entire team. You only have one chance to make a first impression, so make it a good one. We tell our players to sit in the first row in their classes and be on time.

I am a very big stickler for being on time. This is probably my biggest pet peeve. I've left a ton of people behind if they're late for the team bus. I've left players behind for shoot-a-rounds and for trips to the airport. I've even left my assistant coaches behind. After all, I can't treat them differently from the players. So now everyone is usually on the bus a good 10 minutes before departure. On the other hand, if Ruth Riley was late, I would just pretend my watch was wrong! Seriously, there are no exceptions, although I have learned to be more flexible with veteran teams.

I remember one time we had a dinner late in the year and senior Niele Ivey came walking in a half-hour late. I didn't even notice. That team was so mature, and so responsible that we practically threw the rulebook out the window that season. We had rules. We just never had to refer to them because it was a veteran team. Niele came over and said she thought the meal was a half-hour later. She apologized. I told her not to worry about it and to go sit down and eat.

I left two players at Georgetown a couple of years ago: Imani Dunbar and Meaghan Leahy. We were going to the airport to go home. They overslept and missed the bus. They actually beat us to the airport since they had the cab and we had the bus, but you should have seen them. They looked awful. They tell that story now at banquets. I always tell the team to have cab fare, because if they miss the bus, they're on their own. The rule is: if you're late, you come see me, tell me why you're late, and apologize.

We tell them how we would like them to act. You can tell how old your team is by how many rules you have. Our 2001 championship team had five seniors so we didn't need any rules. Everyone knew what was expected of them, and the seniors made sure that the underclassmen followed their lead. Two years ago, with six freshmen, it was a different story. We had to talk about the rules and enforce them. We had five kids miss curfew that season because we arrived at our hotel late, and they went to dinner and got back late. There were consequences because it was a young team, and we have to have that discipline.

I've gotten easier over the years if you ask my former players. They'll tell you I've turned into a cream puff. But ask my current players and they'll tell you I'm very demanding. I don't know that I've gotten easier, but more compassionate, and more understanding certainly. I don't think of myself as a dictator, especially with a seasoned, experienced team.

For example, when we played Connecticut here in 2001 during the championship season, I was more flexible. And that was a huge game that we were fortunate enough to win. Late in the game we were up big, but UConn was firing threes and they hit a couple of them. Well, we were still up by 15 points but I called a 30-second timeout and said, "They're lighting it up, we have to go man-to-man." Niele Ivey said, "No no no . . . we gotta stay in the zone!" Well, they were just exhausted, so I said, "Okay, let's stay in the zone. But will you please go out and guard those shooters?" And Niele said, "I'll think about it." That broke the tension. Niele would have known *not* to do that earlier in her career. But by that point, she was clearly the leader of the team, we had a great relationship, and I respected her opinion. It wasn't a questioning thing in which she was trying to undermine my authority. It was her way of saying, "We're exhausted, Coach."

Compare that to our trip to Italy a couple of years ago where one of our freshman said, "We need to play more man-to-man." You could have heard a pin drop. In that case, I told her, in a not so nice way, that it was not her decision to make. We talked about that later, and I told her when she's a senior, and a leader on the team, she can have some input.

There were times, many times in fact, when I would throw the championship team out of practice and Niele would come by later and say, "You're right, we stunk, what do you want me to do now?" When I throw a *young* team out of practice, nobody comes by later. Ruth and Niele would come by sometimes and just talk about what was working and wasn't.

This was another big change for me as a coach. Early in my career, I would come home and my husband Matt would say, "What did the players think?" I'd say, "I don't know. I didn't ask them. I'm telling them what to think!" Now we have some back and forth, but only with certain players, and only after they've reached a certain point.

Everyone, from players to coaches, is held accountable. We look at a game afterward on film. The players know their roles. We look at the game film and it's *all right there.* There's no looking at anybody else, no blaming anyone else. Look at yourself, and your own game. We talk a lot about looking in the mirror. We win as a team and lose as a team. Always ask, "What can I be doing better?" Some players are extreme about accepting blame. After a loss to Rutgers a couple of years ago, Ruth Riley was saying it was all her fault. I said, "It was not your fault! It was my fault! I should have called a timeout!" When you have a team in which everyone is saying, "It was my fault," you know you have a great group, and probably a pretty good team.

The best players are the ones who hold themselves accountable for their performance. You can tell by a player's comments if she holds herself accountable. This ties into role acceptance. If your role is to score, then you need to score, particularly in a big game. A player has to be willing to say, "I didn't score, or I didn't rebound, like I'm supposed to. And maybe if I had, we would have won the game." If you've accepted your role, then you should think this way. A player has to play to her potential. You can't have a good team until you're good individually first. Too often, though, players will say things like, "They didn't run enough plays for me," or "I didn't get the ball enough," or "The defense was holding me," or "The referees didn't give me the calls." Instead, I want to hear, "I didn't play well enough for us to win."

I guess it's possible to go too far with this and blame yourself for everything and carry the weight of the world on your shoulders. Coaches are like this. Coaches usually take too much responsibility for the way the team plays even though coaches don't have that much control over *how* a team plays. But I think it's okay for coaches to feel this way. Ultimately, responsibility for the season rests with me, and it's my job during the season to beat myself up. For players, however, this can be burdensome and counterproductive.

Teresa Borton is probably the most accountable player we have right now, and she'll give you everything she's got. But still, she'll always say she could have done more. Some of this comes with maturity. Ruth Riley wasn't this way until her junior and senior year. But it's also personality. Megan Duffy, as a freshman, was very accountable. I ask her what she thinks she needs to work on and her response is always "Everything."

This is another one of those coaching challenges. If you try to get a player to own up to her poor performance, that player will feel like you're blaming her for the loss. For example, two years ago we lost to Connecticut badly. Our two leading scorers, Alicia Ratay and Jackie Batteast, went a combined 4 for 25 in shooting. I told the team that our two leading scorers didn't score, and we can't win when that happens. To me, that is verifiable fact, but they thought I blamed them for the loss, and that no one else did anything wrong.

Usually there is enough blame to go around. Sometimes, on the other hand, we play well, but we just lose to a better team. Sometimes the shots just don't go down. This is very difficult for a coach and a team to accept, because it may mean we are just simply not as good as the other team.

Sometimes holding oneself accountable can create another problem. When a player does have a great game, she'll often want the credit for it. After all, if she accepts blame for bad games, she should be entitled to take credit for good games, right? I don't see it that way. I don't give credit when a player has the kind of game she's supposed to have. I'll say she played a great game, but that's it. I won't make a big deal out of it, because that's the kind of game we expect from her. The great players know when they played well, and when they didn't.

Coaches have to be held accountable. After a loss, the coaches will get together, and Carol will blame herself because the post players didn't play well. Coquese will yell at her and say it's the guards' fault, not the post players. Everyone on this staff takes responsibility.

It is tremendously important to use the word *we* as often as possible when addressing the team. This isn't about the coaches or the players. It's about *us*. You lost them as a coach when you start saying *you* did this or *you* didn't do that. We're all in this together. It's also okay as a coach to admit a coaching mistake to the team. I'll say it to the press, so why not to the team? However, I think you have to do this in such a way that you don't undermine the confidence that the team has in you.

That UConn game in 2001 was a good example of where everyone was willing to be held accountable. When everyone takes responsibility, there is no blame. There is trust. Probably because of that trust, I felt really calm before that game. It was a quiet confidence. I really, truly thought we would win that game. We played that game on a Monday. On Saturday before the game, Ruth sprained her ankle and Kelley broke her hand. Everybody thought neither would play. I knew they would. I walked into the arena and an usher stopped me and said, "Did you hear it's a sellout?" I was so excited. My assistants are always telling me, "Don't be nervous. Trust in the players, trust in us, we're going to help you." The players were extremely confident. Our athletic director, Kevin White, always comes into the locker room before the game, but he doesn't stay long because I make him nervous. But I wasn't nervous before this game.

I'm usually a wreck before a game. I don't know why. I always have been. When does it get easier? I asked Homer Drew at Valparaiso that question. He said, "Never. When you stop getting nervous you should probably stop coaching." It's actually worse when you have an opponent you know you should beat, because what if you get beat? I was less nervous playing UConn, because they were *supposed* to win. Kevin White came into the locker room, I was putting on lipstick and I said, "I bet you don't see this when you go in the men's locker room!" I told him how I've waited for this moment my whole life. This is what I dreamed of when I came to Notre Dame. We had a sellout crowd, number one versus number two. I kept telling the team this was the reason we're here.

I hold myself accountable. I second-guess my own coaching, especially after a loss. I can't put a game behind me until I've reviewed the film, read the newspaper, and put together the plan for next practice. I have to know immediately what I did wrong. I don't normally pay much attention to the media, but I do read the *South Bend Tribune*, but only after a loss, not after a win. I don't know why, I guess I just can't put it behind me until I read about it in the newspaper. Occasionally I'll conclude that I wouldn't have done anything differently, but usually I'll find something questionable like why I made a certain substitution, or why I didn't. Why didn't we press, why didn't we go man-to-man? I'm always hardest on myself. I don't think my team knows this because when we lose, nobody talks to me. They used to feel like I didn't like them because we lost, like I was blaming them for the loss. It's not that at all. I'm already thinking about what I did wrong, and how I can fix it. I take a loss pretty hard, and the next day's practice is never pleasant. But after that, I'm fine. I used to hang on to a loss longer than that. Sometimes I'll come into practice and say, "You know what? I burned the tape. I'm not going to make you watch it. Let's move on."

I love practice, I love making up plays, I love planning practice, I love sitting in my office and diagramming plays. I'll be in a restaurant, I'll think of a play and have to draw it on a napkin. I love to put something in, or call something from the sideline, and see it work. To see it executed flawlessly is a huge sense of accomplishment, even though it may only happen once or twice in a game. Then, of course, there are times when something doesn't work, and I'll wonder why, since it looked so good on the napkin! I always think practice is fun. Winning is fun, but even after wins, I would wonder what I could have done better. I've gotten better at enjoying the wins, but it's still about getting back in that gym for practice. Besides, with our schedule, winning and losing doesn't really matter early in the year. It becomes a little more important when conference play begins. I tell the team that March is about winning. Then it is the only thing that matters. But until March, this is only about getting better. I need to feel good about what I'm doing. I need to feel good about being positive and encouraging. If I don't feel that way, even if we win, I don't feel very satisfied.

Players are held accountable, not just to basketball, but to their studies at Notre Dame. The coaches aren't allowed contact with the professors at all. The academic advisor does that, which is why I really don't know very many members of the Notre Dame faculty. We rarely meet. All we can do is encourage the players to do well in class. We know their schedules so we can try to work practice around that, but that's the extent of our involvement. When we're on a bus or plane, the players usually have their books out.

We also have a dress code for road games. The players have to wear skirts, and they hate it. But we look nice when we travel. We'll see some teams in airports, and they'll be in sweats, and our players will say, "Boy, we look good." I want them to be ladies, and I want them to look good because our image is really important. I dress up for games for the same reason. I'm much more comfortable at practices because I can wear sweats. People ask me all the time how difficult it is to coach in heels. Let me tell you, I can move pretty fast in heels. I can even run in heels, and I've done so on occasion to get to the locker room or chase down a player (but never a referee!).

We work with players on addressing the media. One example that comes to mind is Alicia Ratay, who is really, really quiet. ESPN did a special about her. She didn't even want to do it. I told her she should do it because this is something special that she can show her grandchildren someday. Our athletes get trained on dealing with the media, which strikes me as something that might be unique to Notre Dame. We hire a communication specialist from New York who conducts workshops with our players. This consultant puts them through mock interviews in which they work on everything from answering questions to making eye contact with the interviewer.

You can tell in recruiting who is the type of player who will accept responsibility and be accountable. It starts with recruiting kids of good character. You have to trust that they will make good decisions when they are in the dorms or out with friends. You have to make sure they are responsible on and off the court. But their social life takes a back seat to academics and basketball.

Notre Dame has high standards for admission, and sometimes we lose some great athletes because of them. SAT or ACT scores don't always predict success at the college level, and we lose players because we can't get them in. With the changes in NCAA legislation, there are no more partial qualifiers. As a result, you'll be seeing more players playing in their freshman year because of a new sliding scale of eligibility.

We have a sign that reads PRIDE, which stands for Personal Responsibility In Daily Effort. It's the players' job. We make *them* accountable. I give them a list of things to work on in the off-season, and they are supposed to work on that list. If they don't do it, it is obvious when they report in the fall. The player controls attitude and work ethic. She must be self-motivated and improve her weaknesses in the summer.

Players want to be students sometimes, just like other students. They feel like they're missing something in student life by being an athlete, and maybe they are. I think we're very trusting here. For example, we don't have any curfews for our home games. We have 6 A.M. practices and we can tell pretty quickly who was out late. A stamped hand, by the way, is a dead giveaway! We treat them as adults until they prove that they're not. We don't have study hall here. Again, they're responsible to do their homework on their own time. Just don't let the grades slip. If they mess up, they better tell me first, because without a doubt, I will find out. Someone always tells me.

3 DISCIPLINE

Everyone wants to go to heaven,
but nobody wants to die.

—JOE LOUIS

I have found that girls like and prefer structure in their game, probably more so than boys. Girls play grade school basketball, high school ball, maybe even AAU, but they're always in the team setting. They have a coach, a set offense, someone tells them where to go, but they never really learn how to just play the game. Girls are quick to learn how to get from point A to point B, but there's not nearly enough freelance, or *just playing basketball*. If you go by the playgrounds now, you don't see women out there playing basketball. You just don't see them. When I was growing up, it was nine guys and me all the time because we didn't have the opportunity to play on summer teams or AAU. We had to go find a game. Now their time is so taken up by organized ball that when they have the time, they don't want to go find a pickup game because they're trying to get away from basketball. I just think there's too much structure today, especially for girls.

Girls don't watch enough games either. Even with my team, I'll ask the players if they saw the game last night on television. They're watching movies or whatever, and they don't have the mentality that they are students of the game and can learn from watching players and listening to announcers. It takes incredible discipline and dedication for a player to become great. Going out and shooting is good but won't necessarily make you a better basketball player. There is no defense for one thing, and it really doesn't simulate the game. In other words, there is no substitute for just playing.

At the end of the season, we make a list for each of our players on what they need to work on over the summer, and sometimes they just need to play. We tell them to get in the pickup games with guys and just play. AAU and other similarly organized programs have also made the season too long. High school girls are forced to choose between another sport, or AAU, and I don't think that's necessarily good in high school. At many places the season is now year-round. I believe high school athletes should do what they want in the three high school seasons and use the summer to work on their favorite sport. Every player on my team played other sports in high school. Some played golf. Some played softball. But their summers were for basketball.

We can't monitor their summer workouts. We tell them what to work on, and I try to limit it to three things and suggest some drills. But they pretty much do it, or they don't, on their own. Most of them will keep track by logging their workouts; how many shots they take, hit, etc. One of the great frustrations in coaching is when a player comes back in the fall and has not improved in any of the things you'd hoped she'd work on. *We* want them to be good, but *they* have to feel that way too. We'll push them to be the best, but if *they* don't have that desire, it won't matter how *we* feel.

I had one player who I gave the same list to every summer, but she never got any better. She played the same way as a senior that she did as a freshman. She contributed to our national championship, but the next year when she needed to step up and take a leadership role, she didn't know how. She didn't prepare in the summer. One of my favorite quotes is "There will come a time when winter will ask, what did you do all summer?"

This self-discipline is not easy to see in the recruiting process. We have to go with what the high school coaches tell us. We can be fooled because these coaches don't want to hurt a young athlete. We have to ask the right questions, because, as I have said previously, every coach says the same thing, "Hardest worker I ever had, very self-disciplined, a self-starter, a self-motivator." But in high school, the player never gets yelled at and never gets taken out of a game. If she misses 10 shots in a row, the coach yells, "Keep shooting" because she's their only chance to win. Now, they're in college, and they're getting yelled at. They're coming out of the game, and if they miss 10 shots in a row, there's always somebody else on the bench. In fact, they won't be allowed to miss 10 shots in a row. That's where the transition to college becomes very difficult for them.

Many of these high school players are not great defenders. I think they were told to stay out of foul trouble since they were needed in the game. There's not the same intensity or discipline at the high school level. Some girls are the nicest, sweetest ladies *off* the court, but can flip that switch *on* the court. We want players who had tough coaches, who would give them constructive criticism, and who might take them out of a game once in a while. I want to see a player who can handle adversity and can play within the team concept. A player who takes 25 shots a game in high school may not assimilate well into a good college program because she's going to have to share the ball. Although from my experience players who won't share the ball are rare. Typically, we have the opposite problem in women's basketball. That is, women basketball players are usually too *unselfish*.

The biggest disciplinary issue for college athletes anywhere, including Notre Dame, is time management. We don't structure the players' days. We don't like to say they're going to practice from 2 to 4 P.M., then dinner from 5 to 6 P.M., then study table from 7 to 10 P.M. We like to treat them as adults because they have to learn to budget their time. There are three components to college life for these young student-athletes: academics, basketball, and social life. All three are important, but in terms of priority, the social life must always come third.

Social life is easier to find outside of the season, but during the season it's difficult. The trick is to manage these without affecting basketball. If they are struggling in the classroom, eventually that comes out on the basketball floor. They'll be stressed, unfocused, tired, and frustrated. Usually though, it's a problem of time management. They should be able to handle the academics *if* they budget time for it. When I first came to Notre Dame, the coaches were told that if athletes needed to miss a practice to concentrate on academics, that was okay. We were supposed to understand and not penalize them. The problem was that quickly became an excuse for missing practice. I was then being penalized for *their* poor time management, but not anymore. They know the practice schedule well in advance, so there are no excuses. We never let academics be an excuse for poor basketball performance, and at a place like Notre Dame, that would be easy to do.

We've had a lot of players who were disciplined, who found the perfect balance. Probably the best example is Ruth Riley. I would also put Katryna Gaither and Beth Morgan in that group. It's interesting that these are also the best players we've ever had at Notre Dame. Someone like Ruth comes around once in a lifetime: to be the best player in the country and the best student, too? That's pretty unusual.

Of course, our players are human, too, and occasionally have to be reminded of these priorities. We have a program in the academic services area called Intensive Care. We had a player not too long ago who just loved to go out and enjoy herself to the detriment of her academic career. It got to the point where, in consultation with the academic advisor we had to say, "If you miss a class, you miss a game. Period." That worked. And yet, I feel like I'm fairly understanding about the social part. If they're 21, they're responsible adults. We have very few rules about how they conduct themselves in the dorms, and around town. It's not healthy to party too much. You have to sleep and eat right. I remember being a college student, and how much fun that can be. But for my practice, I want them totally focused and ready to play for two hours.

We've been very fortunate here. We haven't had serious problems in this area. It probably starts with recruiting good kids. I can't usually tell which kids are inclined to party, but the campus visit during recruiting can be pretty revealing. The prospect goes out with the girls in the dorm, and we get a pretty good idea of what she's like.

In recruiting, I'm looking for a player who wants to devote the time to improving her game. This is a very big issue. They're playing games and doing AAU, but do they work on their individual game? They might be playing well, and in pretty good shape, and then they have to get in the weight room. It becomes obvious they haven't lifted before. Those kinds of things have to be done *individually*, aside from the team. But weightlifting takes another hour, and it takes discipline.

To be a good shooter, you have to shoot every day. But that also takes another hour. Time commitment has to be such that you're truly dedicated, so when your friends call and say they're going to the mall, you have to be strong enough to say, "Not yet, because I didn't get my workout in." You have to work on your game individually at least five days per week. Shooters should shoot between 200 and 300 shots per day. This is self-discipline.

Ball handling is another individual skill that should be honed. How can any player *not* be a great ball handler? All you need is a ball! This is a great example of just wanting to be good. Anybody, absolutely anybody, can be a great ball handler. That just takes time and effort. It just takes discipline. In fact, there is no excuse for *not* being a great ball handler. We look at these skill levels very closely when recruiting as an indicator of how much individual effort and individual discipline they possess outside of the team structure. And, by the way, parents have no control over this. My son Murphy will not do these drills if *I* tell him to, but *if the kid next door tells him*, he'll go out in the driveway and do them!

Ruth Riley was probably the most disciplined player I ever coached, followed closely by Beth Morgan and Katryna Gaither. On the current team, it would be Teresa Borton. A disciplined player knows where she's supposed to be and is always there. There are players I can ask about the offense, and they can diagram the whole thing. But in a game situation, they're suddenly lost because they don't have the mental discipline to fill their assignment.

Doing the right thing at the right time, all the time, takes a lot of discipline. Consistency is the key. You have to get to the point where you know game after game exactly what you're going to get from every player. We've had talented players who had very little discipline. It's as if their mind doesn't control their body. Obviously, I'd like to have the great athlete who is also disciplined, but without a doubt, I'd rather have the disciplined player who may be marginally athletic than the great athlete who lacks discipline.

At a place like Notre Dame, I think we should be able to find the complete package, the athlete who is disciplined. As a coaching staff, we talk about this all the time, but you'd be surprised how rare this combination actually is. For some reason, we cannot find the player who can defend *and* shoot the ball. I'm now convinced there is no such animal. For some reason, every shooter seems to be a slow kid.

They believe they're shooters, so they work on their shot, not their defense. Faster athletes, on the other hand, work on beating people off the dribble and slashing to the basket, so they're not great shooters. Niele Ivey is the closest we've ever come to a player who could shoot *and* defend. So we try to recruit shooters and defenders and blend them somehow on the floor. It's really hard to take a good defender and make her into a good shooter. Likewise, it's hard to make a shooter into a great defender. This is why we play a lot of zone. We can hide one poor defender, but not more than one.

Coaches also have to be willing to discipline players. I like rules. I grew up with rules. If there is one rule that is my favorite, it's punctuality. I'm a stickler for being on time. If a player is late, the whole team runs. If a player misses any appointment, a practice, a meeting with the academic advisor, whatever, she gets a 6 A.M. appointment with the strength and conditioning coach. It's important to treat everyone the same. I can't wait three extra minutes for Ruth Riley to get on the bus, if I don't give three extra minutes to everyone else. I don't set rules that I can't enforce. For example, I don't set curfews in the dorm. I really can't check on that, but I think it's important to have some rules. If a player misses curfew on the road, she won't start the next game. Players are fine with rules if they know them in advance. The problem comes when a coach says you're in trouble if you're late, and we'll decide the punishment when it happens. Then you're likely to have different punishments for different kids, and that's a problem.

You learn to discipline through experience, too. I've had players who were problems. I've suspended some players. I've had players attempt to undermine my efforts, and sometimes they were successful. We've had dissension on certain teams. Any disciplinary measures I take, I do so with the team's best interest in mind. It helps to have great team leaders, because they can keep the other players in line, and make my job as disciplinarian much easier.

With this young team I can already see some leaders emerging. One of them could be Katy Flecky, or Jackie Batteast. Another is Teresa Borton. The biggest attribute of a leader is the willingness to do what's right, even if the rest of the team doesn't see it that way. You have to be willing to take a stand. You have to be willing to tell your team-mate, one of your friends, that she isn't working hard. A lot of players, especially women, have trouble telling their friends this because women want to be liked. And players, especially women players, are very sensitive. Nobody likes to be criticized, and nobody likes to be criticized in front of someone else. I have to watch this as a coach. I tell them to listen to *what* I say, not *how I say it*. And women hold a grudge. They get upset after you've jumped all over them, where I think guys tend to shrug it off and play. I really have to be careful about that. If you ever watch me coach, when I'm walking away from a player I just pulled out of a game, it's because I have to, otherwise I'm going to jump all over that player, and that can be counterproductive. I always try to high-five them when they come out of a game, but sometimes I'm afraid I'll say something I'm going to regret, so I walk away to the end of bench and take a deep breath. That's how you know when I'm angry.

The best leader we ever had was Beth Morgan, because she wanted to win, and that was it. In order to win, she would do anything including telling her teammates to pick it up. You have to be the hardest worker. The leader has to do extra work. Maybe she comes to practice a little early, and stays a little late. Unfortunately, I think, you also have to be a pretty good player to be a leader. We've had some players with leadership qualities, but didn't play enough to assume the role of leader. So I make them the bench captain. Karen Swanson and Imani Dunbar were two great bench captains.

Confidence is the number one issue with women in general, and with women basketball players too. To my amazement, this is true even at Notre Dame. I tell them, "You are at *Notre Dame!* You are obviously a great student, and a great athlete! How can you not have confidence?" The fact is, they need constant reinforcement. It's a big part of our job, and one I didn't understand early in my coaching career. A player would say, "I've lost my confidence." I used to think, "Sit down and I'll play someone who has it!" You can tell a player four things she did well and one thing she did not. She'll react to the one thing she didn't do well. There's a *way* to say things that can make all the difference in the world. Unfortunately, I'm still learning what that way is.

Discipline is really evolutionary in many ways. With a young team you need to be more of a disciplinarian. Clearly, they need that direction. But at the same time, you want to give every opportunity to the seniors to emerge as the leaders. So I'm constantly negotiating how much discipline is necessary for a particular team. The year after we won the championship, I made a decision about halfway through that season that I was going to play the freshmen ahead of some upperclassmen. In retrospect, I probably should have said that from the beginning of the season because they were playing better than the upperclassmen. But I was afraid of what that might do to the team chemistry and morale. I didn't think the upperclassmen were mature enough to handle a freshman playing ahead of them. The upperclassmen didn't have a good attitude, and they destroyed our team chemistry. Eventually, it became clear that the freshmen were taking over the team, and I was in favor of that and allowed it to happen.

That clearly created a division. There were players who just couldn't accept that the freshmen were better. Some veteran players spent the summer polishing their championship rings instead of improving their games and believed that by virtue of being an upperclassman they would automatically start *and* become the next Ruth Riley or Niele Ivey. It doesn't work that way. You have to earn it. No doubt it hurt our chemistry, but this group will rally and put it together. I think sometimes you have to go through a bad experience like that to make the team stronger. Like Ruth Riley her junior year, when she vowed not to go through another bad year, I think the freshmen said they didn't want to go through that again. That year just wasn't a lot of fun. And I think each year this group will improve. You can learn a lot in a down year, as a player and a coach. It can ultimately make you stronger. I'm not sure we win a national championship without the turbulent season before it. It's definitely easier to build to a national championship than to maintain it, and I looked at that bad season as part of the building process.

4 RESPECT AND LOYALTY

When we become part of anything,
It becomes part of us.

— DAVID HAROLD FINK

You cannot have a successful team if players don't respect each other and the coaches. This works both ways—the coaches have to have respect for the players, too. Respect is earned, but there should also be a certain level of respect for every human being whether or not you know him or her.

You also have to respect your opponents. We respect our opponents always, sometimes too much, sometimes too little. It's easy to disrespect an opponent that you should beat handily. I don't know if you can guard against that kind of letdown. As a coach, I feel like we approach every game the same, with total respect for our opponent. But players are players. They are young, and they read the papers. In other words, they know when they're supposed to win. Sometimes they'll let up in a game because of it. This is the lack of killer instinct, which I think is more personality than maturity. You either have this or you don't, and here's where a deep bench can help you. Good players, itching for the chance to play, can come in and put a game away for you, or at least sustain the lead. Without a good bench, it's hard to substitute when you have a lead, for fear of losing it.

So much of this job has become psychology. It used to be about basketball. Things have changed. The coach used to command respect by virtue of the position. He or she was allowed to be authoritarian and a disciplinarian. And the parents used to back the coach. Today everyone seems to be treated so carefully, so fragilely, always concerned about self-esteem. Let's let everyone win. Let's give everyone a medal or trophy. You know what? I have a lot of trouble understanding this as a coach. In life, not everyone will win, and not everyone can be the star. I'm not the nurturing type of coach and, in fact, no one on our coaching staff is, either. Next time I hire an assistant, I may need to hire someone who is compassionate, if such a coach exists!

A lot of this is mental toughness. Some kids will never become mentally tough because of how they were raised, but I've seen some grow tremendously in this area. In our program, I thought Ruth Riley was a little soft when she arrived here. She was frustrated because she was getting fouled a lot, and I think she had to make a choice. She could either give up or accept that she's going to get beat up and resign herself to getting mentally tougher. Obviously, she decided to get mentally tougher. Kelley Siemon played a season with a broken hand. There was never a doubt she would play, but sometimes I wonder how many kids would play through an injury like that today. I think every player gets to a point where she has to decide, "Am I going to continue to make excuses, or am I going to step up and play?"

By the way, I don't like players questioning the referee, because it's a sign of disrespect, but the players expect *me* to question the referees. If I don't question them the players think everyone, including me, is against them. I don't believe in getting a technical foul just to fire the team up, and, in fact, I've only had two technicals since I've been at Notre Dame. I don't think ranting and raving on the sidelines accomplishes much, and I have to role model my behavior for the team. The players are going to play like I coach. If I scream at the referees, the players will think it's okay for them to do it, too.

Respect between players and coaches is critical. If players don't think their coaches know what they're doing— or worse, if the players don't think the coaches care about them—there will be trouble. We talk to players about mutual respect. I respect all my players as people. I have had players that I've had trouble respecting—as players. The quickest way for someone to lose my respect as a player is for that player to put out minimal effort. I have trouble respecting anyone who doesn't work hard. It's also difficult for me to respect anyone who tries to undermine the team, and, unfortunately, it only takes one player with a bad attitude to destroy team chemistry.

Sometimes players don't realize what a two-way street this is. They assume that the coaches should automatically respect them for their high school accomplishments, and that it's a privilege for us to coach them. Most players think they are a joy to coach despite the problems they cause. Even after graduation, they forget the problems they caused while they were here. Having a short memory is probably a good attribute for a coach to possess.

It's not uncommon for players to blame coaches when things don't go their way. Unfortunately, it is the culture we live in to blame someone else for our problems. Coaches will continue to get fired for losing games, and players will never take responsibility for contributing to those losses.

There have been so many players who have come through here that I have tremendous respect for, and sometimes it's not the people you think. One example is Karen Swanson, who played from 2000 to 2003. I have tremendous respect for her. She was never a star here, but a very hard worker. Jill Krause, a current team member, is another. On the championship team, I had great respect for Imani Dunbar and Meaghan Leahy. These are players that helped us win without getting a lot of time on the court. I guess I sometimes have more respect for people who have had some bad breaks yet have persevered and contributed.

Always respect your opponents. There are schools with no academic standards, and there are programs that break the rules, but for the most part the women's game still has a lot of integrity. If you don't respect an opponent, you'll get beat. We fear no opponents, but we respect all of them.

It is much more important to be respected than to be liked, and here again is a fundamental issue with female

athletes especially. Women want to be liked. I want players to believe me and have confidence in what I'm saying.
It really doesn't matter if they like me. Of course, ideally
we want to be respected *and* liked. But if it's one or the
other, I'll take respect any day.

Assistant coaches can get closer to the players than head
coaches, and they are usually well liked. In fact, it used to
bother me that some players were closer to my assistants
than they were to me. As the head coach, you sit on top of
the hierarchy, and I couldn't understand why players
wouldn't just come and talk to me. They would, however,
talk to the assistants. There were times when I thought being
an assistant coach would be a fun job. You have none of the
pressure, but all of the fun. I never thought of myself as
unapproachable, but I had to learn that the whole relationship is just different. As the head coach, I guess I'm more of
a mom to the players, while the assistant coaches are more
like sisters. There are things you'd tell your sister that you
wouldn't tell your mom. This used to bother me some, but
it's a relationship I've come to like and appreciate.

Another issue closely tied to respect is loyalty. You don't
see loyalty as much anymore, but it's very important to me.
You don't see it in society. People change jobs all the time,
and it's creeping into athletics. If a player isn't happy, she
transfers. There is no loyalty at all. There is none. It's all
about "me," and that's a bad thing. Just look each year at
the number of athletes transferring. It's staggering. I feel
betrayed by a transfer who I was counting on to fill a spot
for us. If she leaves, there's going to be a big hole and I can't
do a thing about it. Depending on the class, and the time
of year of the transfer, it can take a couple of years to fill the

hole left by a transfer. Then of course, other coaches will use that transfer as a negative recruiting tactic against us.

Transfers hurt us in other ways too. It hurts our reputation. It hurts our graduation rate too, even though the transfer will end up graduating from some school. But she won't graduate from Notre Dame, and that counts against *our* graduation rate. Players need to be loyal not just to the coaches, but to the institution. My players need to be loyal to the University of Notre Dame.

For some reason, I've noticed that there is more loyalty with coaches in the women's game than in the men's. If you look around women's college basketball, you'll find coaches who have been at the same institution for a long time. Men tend to jump around a little more looking for better jobs. I may be totally off saying this, but I don't think women are that motivated by money. I think women are much more motivated by security and a comfortable working environment.

I feel very loyal to Notre Dame. I love this institution and what it stands for. When I first arrived here, I had a lot of growing to do as a coach. Notre Dame helped me through those years, and we're finally reaping the benefits of that. They stood by me while I was gaining experience, and now that I have that, I feel a need to give back to Notre Dame.

I got a call from an athletic director last year who wanted me to consider coaching at his institution. I told him no thanks. I already have the best job in America. Three other candidates told him the exact same thing. There tends to be a lot of job satisfaction for coaches in this game, and we're lucky to feel this way.

5 PRACTICE DOESN'T MAKE PERFECT

The harder you work, the harder it is to surrender.

—VINCE LOMBARDI

It's not true that practice makes perfect. Actually the saying should be "perfect practice makes perfect." It's not just about effort. You have to have effort and *intelligence*. We talk quite a bit about that. This is especially true when I see a player who could be great defensively. She has great energy and enthusiasm, but she fouls or is out of place guarding the wrong person. It's a combination of effort and the intelligence to stay within the team concept and know exactly what everyone on the team is supposed to be doing.

Great players work more individually outside of practice than the average players. The really great players are the ones who come in early, stay late, and come in on their day off. Beth Morgan, Ruth Riley, and Katryna Gaither are examples, and it's obvious why they were the best players. They knew their weaknesses, and they worked on those weaknesses. We've had good players who came in and worked hard in practice. But after those two hours are over, they leave. The only way you can improve as a player is by what you do on your own. To that extent, I believe players are made over the summer. If you put the time in over the summer, when the coaches aren't allowed to be there, that's when you really see the improvement. It's very evident who put in the extra effort.

We've had people who have left the locker room after having just played a game and go straight to our auxiliary gym, the pit, to shoot free throws because they weren't happy with the way they shot them during the game. You have to have that kind of dedication to be great. Our players, no doubt, missed out on a lot in high school. While their friends were at the mall, they were playing basketball. It takes a great deal of sacrifice to be good, let alone great.

Practice has always been my favorite part of coaching. I look forward to practice. Always. After the UConn win in 2001, I gave them a day off. But I also told the team that practices were going to get tougher so we wouldn't get complacent. The team understood because that was a team with a great attitude.

Practice always seems to go fast. Our practices involve a ton of preparation. At the end of the season, we begin preparing practices for next year. We review our offenses and defenses. We watch a lot of game film. Then we try to decide, based on which players will be returning, what will work and what won't next season. We might talk about introducing new things depending on our personnel. It's important to do this because we can then spend the summer learning. We visit coaches and we go to clinics. If we think we'll be able to press in the upcoming season, for example, I'll assign an assistant coach to go visit Rick Pitino to learn more about presses. In other words, for coaches, summer is for homework.

We'll come back in September and I'll develop a master plan. I'll lay out the offenses and we'll prioritize. Which ones do we introduce first? Opponents dictate this. Defensively, what will be our philosophy? I don't think you can be good at all offenses and defenses, so we simplify. And I don't think you can introduce more than one thing per day, so we try to measure what we accomplish daily. Defensively, most teams are either zone or man-to-man type teams. We play a lot of zone, but you have to be a good man-to-man team to play a good zone, so we do work on man-to-man principles, but we'll concentrate on zones.

The coaching staff meets every morning at 9 A.M. to plan practice for later in the day. Sometimes that involves breaking down film from a game the night before. We probably spend about an hour planning the practice. We plan one day at a time and it's structured down to the minute, although I also have a master monthly calendar to remind me of things we need to get to, and when. One day we may work exclusively on man-to-man defense. The next day it might be zone. We try to have one thing we want to emphasize for the day. Sometimes it's intensity or communication, and sometimes it's a specific part of the offense or defense. We try to keep practices short, maybe to two hours, which may not seem short, but it is. We'll spend two hours from stretching to finish, but we maximize those two hours. The players actually determine the length of practice. I'll tell them that if they get it right in the amount of time we've scheduled, it could be a shorter practice. If they don't get it right, we might be there all night. With a young team, these practices can get very long. With a veteran team, we can usually shorten them. In fact, with the national championship team, we got into a cycle where we would practice for an hour and a half, play a game, then take a day off. You might think the opposite to be true; that to be that good you have to practice all the time. On the contrary, if you practice efficiently, you don't have to practice as often.

We work hard in practice. The team's work ethic will give you a clue as to how successful the team will be. Some teams will rest at certain points in practice. Some will save their energy for March, but if you pace yourself during the season you may not be playing in March! You really have to learn how to work hard, and then do it consistently throughout the season. This is a big adjustment for freshmen. One of our current players, Courtney LaVere, told me how different—and how much easier—it was in high school. She commented that she didn't have to be at her best every minute. At our practices, she finds she has to play at her best and as hard as she can, every single minute, because the competition is so much better.

I keep a record of practices. I have records of practices going back several years. It's useful to be able to go back to remind myself of what I've addressed in practice and what I haven't. Every practice and every drill should have a goal, and a consequence for failing to reach that goal. Nothing motivates like running. If we fail to reach a goal, we run, and that's always been a pretty good incentive. The coaches have assignments. We're all looking at different things, different players. In scrimmages, I try to keep my starters together. After all, they're going to play together in games. At the same time, there will be substitutions, foul trouble, and injuries during the season, so I don't want to play the top five in practice together all the time.

A good practice is one in which players are mentally sharp, focused, and I didn't have to repeat myself. A good practice is short, but intense and efficient. Duration is a good indicator of a successful practice. If practice is short, then we got it done.

We look at tapes of all of our opponents. We usually get about five tapes for each opponent. Each coach is assigned an opponent, breaks down the tapes, and creates a highlight tape. We look at the opponent's tendencies. We try to guess what they'll try to do to us.

I base our defenses and offenses on our opponent, and on the type of players we have. Trying to guess what our opponent is going to do to us is a big part of our game plan. We play our conference opponents more than once usually, so we know them pretty well. We don't focus so much on our opponents' overall schemes and philosophies as much as their players' individual tendencies. For example, we may notice that a certain opposing player likes to drive baseline, so we work on shutting off the baseline in practice. We might notice that another player is left-handed, so we'll work on forcing that player to go to her right. Players seem to play to their same tendencies, but a team may change its plays on us. So preparing too much against a team's offenses and defenses can be a waste of time if that team decides to change what they've been doing all year.

Our strategy is also dictated by our personnel. With Ruth Riley, I didn't want her in foul trouble, and I wanted her around the basket, so zone defense made sense. Of course, all the preparation is worthless if players don't execute. We can preach to players to challenge an opponent's shot, and sometimes we don't get it done and our opponent will torch us for 30 points. To the fans, we probably look unprepared. We're always prepared, we just don't always execute.

We take one game at a time. We never look ahead, and we never look past weaker opponents to more imposing games down the road. Even with all of the preparation, you have to be flexible. We've gone into games thinking there is no way we can play this team man-to-man, and five minutes into the game we switch to man-to-man!

We don't spend a lot of time in practice on traditional conditioning. If we go hard in the drills and in scrimmages, that is conditioning. But we don't spend a lot of time just running. There shouldn't be a need. If you work hard in practice, you will be in game shape. We do use running as motivation in that every one of our drills has goals, and the consequence of failing to reach those goals is to run. For example, we may need to shoot 70 percent on a particular offensive drill, or we may need two stops on a defensive drill. If we don't meet those goals, we run. That works well if players know the consequences in advance. Sometimes we'll keep a tally in practice. For example, we may tell them defensively they must accomplish three things: box out, front the post, and keep the ball out of the middle. After practice, we'll get the tally from the manager, and they may have to run 20 sprints. Hopefully, we'll have fewer and fewer sprints as the season goes on. It's important that you hold the whole team responsible for mistakes. Sometimes players are more motivated to work hard if they know they're letting the team down.

I would say our practices aren't as hard physically as they are mentally. In fact, it is my goal to make practices mentally tough. When you get into games, you really need the mental toughness. At times the crowd will be into it, the calls will go against you, and you really need to be mentally strong. I'll tell my players before practice that this practice will challenge them mentally, and that I don't want to win this battle. Then, we make it tough. We call a lot of fouls. Sometimes we make stuff up. We'll tell them they have to run the offense five times in a row without turning the ball over, with someone getting back for transition defense and three rebounders in the lane. Or they may have to make five passes before a shot goes up. We might tell them they need to make three out of five shots. By comparison, then, the game is easier because it's less challenging mentally than practice.

Practice is important, too, because I believe execution is crucial, especially if you don't have great athletes. Athleticism is probably more important on defense than on offense. For example, Beth Morgan and Alicia Ratay could execute offenses. Those two might be the best I've ever seen at reading screens. Neither one of them was particularly fast, but they could score on defenders who were much quicker because they were smart.

Attention to detail is critical for success, and this is something else we emphasize every day and every practice. On the offense, each player has to be in a certain spot so that we have good spacing around the floor. We move them inches on the court sometimes, if that's what it takes to get them in the right spot to get the correct angle to make the correct pass or take the correct shot. The same is true defensively. It is really important that everyone is in the right place. We stress this in everything including running wind sprints in which we make sure everyone touches the lines. Those drills carry over to the games, so we pay attention to the little things. In the end, this is the difference between good teams and great teams. Good teams will get sloppy because they don't pay attention to detail in practice. Great teams do the little things well.

It is a myth to believe that we don't stress the fundamentals in practice every day. People probably believe that at this level these athletes are fundamentally sound. They should be, but they aren't. In fact, some of them learn poor habits in high school because they are so talented they don't have to have good fundamentals. We have to practice rebounding, particularly boxing out, and we spend a lot of time on footwork. These kids were so good in high school that they didn't have to box out. They could rebound over their opponents. Defensively, if a player gets by her, she's good enough in high school to recover and block the shot from behind. These are bad habits that can get you by in high school when you're the best athlete on the floor, but it won't work at this level. We literally have to retrain them, which is hard because they're older now and set in their ways. It always amazes me how some of the great players actually know very little about the fundamentals. This is frustrating for a coach because my first inclination is to install the offense and defense and go five on five. Then I look at the skills and realize we have to start with fundamentals. I'm talking about ball handling skills, using your left hand, triple threat position, boxing out, staying low defensively. These are the same things every high school coach in America is talking about. Any player that comes to us with these skills is a bonus, but I don't expect it.

Another part of our preparation for the season is scheduling exhibition games. Of course we scrimmage among ourselves, but the problem with intersquad games is both teams know the offenses and defenses. In other words, they can cheat! With exhibition games you can see if your schemes really work. There is also a lot to be said about getting a team in its uniforms and getting the players in front of a crowd. This is especially important for freshmen, who will naturally be nervous. Exhibition games allow you to answer, "Where are we?" We can compare ourselves to last year at the same time, and we can compare to where we need to be by March. We find out the positives in exhibition games, and the negatives will become the focus of practice.

Preparation for exhibition games is very different, too. There is no scouting report on our opponent. Two years ago, one of the teams pressed us before we even had a press offense installed. We meet in the gym, the pit, about two hours before the game and run through our plays without defense. Normally, we would also run through our opponents' plays, but without a scouting report that's not possible for an exhibition game. Don't think the outcome of an exhibition game is unimportant. We play to win. It's important to come out with confidence early in the year, and this is especially important with young teams.

Something else we do in practice is scrimmage against male basketball players. These guys are students here, they are good athletes, and they have to be certified. They basically get the same treatment as our players. They get sent through the same academic advising. They have to maintain their eligibility. They watch film with us so they can simulate our opponents. We started this several years ago when we had a lot of injuries. We only had eight players, and it was too late to take walk-ons. You can't scrimmage with eight. One of the girl's boyfriends showed up to practice with her, and then one of his friends came, and the next thing you knew, we had a team. We also had two weddings!

Our players pick these guys. They go to the Rec Center, and to the Bookstore Basketball Tournament and they scout. We also go to the tryouts for the men's team to see who they cut, and try to get them to come out. We end up usually with about six guys who are really good players, they match up to us pretty well and essentially function as a scout team for us. We have a couple of them who are about six-foot-three to match up with our posts, and some guards who can shoot and defend. This works well for everybody. The women take out their frustrations on the guys, rather than each other. The guys enjoy playing, and our team gets to stay together rather than having to divide them all the time. For me, it means I can play my top six or seven together. These guys are really good players. In fact, during the championship season, our team never beat the guys once in practice. I remember a reporter asking Ruth Riley how it felt to be undefeated and she told him we lose every day in practice! I also have the team set the goals for the season. The players do this. I want these to be *their* goals. We meet in the locker room before the season and I ask them what they want to do this season, and how far they want to go. It's interesting to hear what the players say. Some are very goal oriented, while others just want to win. In 2001, one of our goals was to win the Big East. We weren't picked to win it, but the players thought we should win it. Another goal was to get further in the NCAA Tournament than we did the year before. Other goals are very specific so that we can measure them. For example, one of the goals was to shoot 50 percent from the field and 70 percent from the line. We want to make more free throws than the other team takes. We want a positive assist-to-turnover ratio. We want fewer than 15 turnovers per game while forcing more than 22 turnovers from our opponent. We want to hold the opponent to fewer than nine offensive rebounds and prevent any single player from having a big night against us. These can all be measured statistically.

More general goals include maximum effort every day. This is more difficult to measure, but the coaches know, and so do the players. We can show them the film. The film is very important here as an objective measurement. It's very hard to accuse someone of poor effort without evidence, because the player will contend that she is playing hard. Even with the film, a player will often contend that she is playing hard, or that the film caught one isolated instance.

For additional evidence, I've been known to spring the pop quiz on them. They're used to taking tests, so this is not a problem for them. I'll quiz them on our offenses and defenses, mainly to see where I've failed in teaching them. But I'll also ask them to name the three hardest workers on the team, and then we share the results. Last year, we had three players who didn't get named at all. At the next practice, those three practiced harder than I've ever seen. It reinforced what the coaches already knew, and it's sometimes more powerful coming from teammates than from us. I don't do that often, because you have to be sure of how those who don't get named will react. This has the potential to divide and cause friction, so I don't do this until I'm sure of the team chemistry. We also expect a positive attitude, which is rarely a problem around here.

The challenge in setting goals is finding the balance between being realistic and, yet, not selling the team short—which of course thinks it can win every game. This is a psychological challenge for any coach, which is why I let *the team* set the goals. If the goal is totally unrealistic, it creates a lot of pressure, frustration, and disappointment when the goal isn't achieved. Sometimes the goal is set too low, which is also a challenge for the coach. Two years ago, for example, the team set the goal of getting to the Sweet 16 in the tourney. Personally, I thought we could do better, but I stayed quiet and let the team talk it out. As they continued to set goals they mentioned winning the out-of-conference games and the Big East. It became apparent to them that if they achieve those goals, they could do better than the Sweet 16. So that goal was raised without the need of any interference from me. The goal is received better if someone else other than the coach says it. This is where team captains come into play. They should take the leadership role in setting goals, and they do.

6 WHY COMPETE?

The most important thing in life is not the triumph,
but the struggle.

—BARON PIERRE DE COUBERTIN

There is a myth that only men are competitive and that women don't need competition. I've always thrived on competition. I've always been competitive in everything from checkers to who can get the dishes done the fastest. It's the running joke in my family. My sisters are all competitors. We were once pulling weeds at my mom's house, and suddenly we realized we were keeping track of the number of bags we filled!

But this is a good thing for women, and society is just beginning to accept that it's okay for women to be competitive. The things we learn from sports do help us tremendously in other areas of our lives. We learn about discipline, teamwork, and how to have a great work ethic. We learn how to be determined, how to persevere, and to never give up. We learn that it's okay to lose, so long as you lose while giving your best effort. I'm still struggling with accepting losing. I just try not to let my team see it.

If you get into corporate work, particularly as a female, sports can only help you. It's still a man's world. It's getting better, but there are still too many places where women are in the minority. Sports help you to learn how to deal with that. These lessons are long-term lessons, and I'm sure no teenager has ever looked this far ahead. We try to show our players the long-term application. We try to show them how these lessons will help them down the road, but down the road for them is next week! To them, 30 is old! They can't think that far ahead, so it's not until they get out and look back where they see the value of competing. I've talked to former players who have been through some adverse situations in life, and they've credited their background in sports with helping them through.

We teach our players that they can be anything they want to be. That's one of the reasons I enjoy the position I'm in. I'm a female coach, and, yet, I have a family. So, I'm evidence that women can have a career and a family. It doesn't have to be a choice. I realize that this thrusts me into the category of role model, but I'm okay with that.

Being a man and having a demanding job can be very stressful. I find that I have much more stress at home than I do at the office. I simply don't have time to do everything I need to do at home. For example, sometimes I think my son, Murphy, grows overnight! Suddenly, it seems, one morning his pants are too tight or too short, and we

Katryna Gaither, left, and Beth Morgan, middle, were instrumental in pushing our program to the next level. (Photo by Donny Crowe, courtesy of Sports Information Department, University of Notre Dame)

I'm not sure what emotion I'm feeling here, but people who say I'm calm during a game simply don't know me very well. (Photo by Mike Bennett, courtesy of Sports Information Department, University of Notre Dame)

Ruth Riley shoots the first of two game-winning free throws against Purdue to win the national championship in 2001. (Photo courtesy of Sports Information Department, University of Notre Dame)

Alicia Ratay is the NCAA leader in 3-point shooting percentage in a four-year period, and yet had to be encouraged to shoot. (Photo by Mike Bennett, courtesy of Sports Information Department, University of Notre Dame)

The coaches are clearly calm and unconcerned here. From left that's Carol Owens, me, Coquese Washington, and Kevin McGuff (Photo by Mike Bennett, courtesy of Sports Information Department, University of Notre Dame)

Beth Morgan was much like me in terms of personality, and she led us to our first Final Four appearance (Photo by Matt Cashore)

Ruth Riley handled the media attention in the NCAA tourney with unbelievable grace and poise. (Photo by Matt Cashore)

Point guard is the most important position on the team and Niele Ivey was one of the best. (Photo by Matt Cashore)

When we recruited Katryna Gaither, her father said she would be an All-American. He was right. (Photo by Matt Cashore)

Here I am again retaining my composure during a calm moment. (Photo by Mike Bennett, courtesy of Sports Information Department, University of Notre Dame)

The attention from being ranked number 1 was overwhelming. I was completely unprepared for it. (Photo courtesy of Sports Information Department, University of Notre Dame)

This team won a national championship because these players unselfishly accepted their roles. (Photo by Matt Cashore)

In addition to being a great player, Beth Morgan might be the best leader I've ever coached. (Photo by Matt Cashore)

Ruth Riley celebrates with Meaghan Leahy after the national championship game in 2001. While their roles were very different, they were equally important. (Photo by Matt Cashore)

Chemistry on the coaching staff is just as important as team chemistry. With me from left are Kevin McGuff, Coquese Washington, and Carol Owens. (Photo by Mike Bennett, courtesy of Sports Information Department, University of Notre Dame)

It's unusual to find women basketball players who don't mind posting down low and playing a physical brand of basketball. Ruth Riley was obviously the exception. (Photo by Matt Cashore)

We were going to wait until the very end of recruiting for Jacqueline Batteast to commit to Notre Dame. She was a local high school star whom we felt we had to have in our program. (Photo by Matt Cashore)

It's nice to see hard work pay off, and few players worked harder than Ruth Riley. (Photo courtesy of Sports Information Department, University of Notre Dame)

Being a coach at Notre Dame is a highly visible position, but I also know I'm lucky to be here. (Photo by Mike Bennett, courtesy of Sports Information Department, University of Notre Dame)

My husband Matt and son Murphy give me perspective by reminding me that basketball is just a game. (Photo courtesy of Sports Information Department, University of Notre Dame)

need to go shopping. But I'm on my way to the airport to go recruiting. Or sometimes he has a school project due, or three exams coming up, and I'm away with the team. I never really thought I'd be good as a stay-home mom, because I love my job. But I also have trouble shaking the guilty feeling that I could have done more for Murphy. I've missed some of his basketball and soccer games, and I really hate that and wonder how I can make it up to him. Women have to make tough choices, but at least we have choices.

Most of my players played for men in high school and in AAU, so playing for me is unusual for them. And it's unusual in society. Here's an example: there are times that my husband, Matt, accompanies me to high school games, and someone once complained that he was involved in recruiting! If Notre Dame men's coach Mike Brey took his wife, Tish, to a game, I'm sure no one would say a word. The assumption is that since she is a woman she is disinterested in sports, and, therefore, doesn't know as much as he does about basketball.

It's really interesting how the two games, men's and women's, are perceived. We've been fighting perception for decades. I hear how male coaches talk to their teams, how they talk to referees, and I watch their sideline behavior. Players react differently to male versus female coaches. Men get away with a lot more because players expect men to be direct, honest, and not as compassionate. The players don't read into things a male coach tells them as much as they do when a female coach yells at them. Women and men are perceived differently, and we have a long way to go to reach equality. Women are supposed to be nurturing and compassionate. That has never been me. I tend to be demanding and direct, which probably surprises a lot of people because I go against the stereotype.

The fact is women are still judged in this culture by their appearance. I see this everywhere we go. The things fans say, they would never say to guys. I have an attractive team, and it's amazing how many people think that's important. My players notice that, too, and, yet, I can't imagine a men's team saying, "Well, at least we're better looking!" But that's my point. It does matter to women, and it shouldn't.

I want my players to be ladies off the court, which is why we have a dress code. They wear dresses when we travel because image is important. They are athletes, but they are also women. We do talk about image a lot, and etiquette. I want them to represent our program in a first-class way.

I've always had a man on my coaching staff because I know in certain situations he could get away with more in terms of coaching our team. Our players almost expect him to rant and rave and show less compassion. If he says to one of our players, "You stunk," she would probably agree and go play. If *I* say, "You stunk," she takes it personally and holds it against me. Of course, some players react better to certain styles of coaching. I remember Beth Morgan telling me, "You don't need to tell me when I play well, I know when I play well, and when I don't." She was low maintenance—a coach's dream! She was very direct, very much like me, which is probably why we went to the Final Four her senior year. Ruth Riley was like that, too. She didn't need a lot of attention. The great players are usually low maintenance. They know when they played well, or played poorly. They don't require a lot of attention from the coaches. They just do their job, and they are usually their own worst critics.

Even though I enjoy competition, I also know that competition can be unhealthy. Win at all costs is unhealthy. There has to be a balance that you learn as a coach. When I first started coaching, it was all about winning. I was obsessed with it. I yelled a lot, and I thought every possession was life and death. That quickly becomes a negative. There have been times when I'm embarrassed by my own behavior. Two years ago, Jackie Batteast was hurt and we lost in the first round of the Big East Tournament, the only time that has ever happened. I went in the locker room after that game and just exploded. I went on a 10-minute rant in which I questioned everything from their effort to their pride. The message, although I didn't say it, was *how could you do this to me?* The next day I couldn't believe I did that. And now I had to get them ready for the next game. I've finally realized that it's more important *how* we played, rather than whether we won or lost.

I don't *de-emphasize* winning. I definitely want to win; it's just not the most important thing. This is a very difficult perspective to keep in mind because our culture emphasizes winning. Everyone from the fans, to the media, to the players expects us to win. And it is true that winning will answer all of them, but it still comes down to looking at oneself in the mirror. You might win every game but not be happy with yourself and the way you treated people along the way. Winning them all is not my measure of a great year. We've had seasons in which we've won a lot of games but had an awful experience.

It really is true that it's not whether you win or lose, but how you play the game. But this isn't so much about sportsmanship as much as playing well and improving. You have to feel good about the way you play because you can't gain confidence from playing poorly. Confidence is fragile until you play well. And this can become cyclical. You can't gain confidence until you play well, but you can't play well without confidence, either.

Players need to know you believe in them, especially when they are playing poorly. It's hard for a coach to know when to give confidence to a player who is struggling, and when to give someone else a chance. Your job as a coach is to put your best team on the floor, but you need to give players on the bench confidence, too. You have to be a good communicator to accomplish this.

Winning should not be a factor at all in youth sports, especially grade school basketball. Wanting to win and playing hard are important, but if kids give their best effort and still lose, so what? Kids need to feel good about the effort, not bad about losing. I believe everybody should get in the game at that level, too. There is plenty of time in the future where the best players will play. Grade schools should be training grounds for teaching the fundamentals and developing an interest in sports. Young athletes should be taught about sportsmanship (I must have missed that chapter!), effort, and intensity. They should be learning how to compete, with confidence. That's the coaches' job at that level.

I know how early these sports start, too, and people frequently ask me if this is good for children. I know of Biddy Basketball leagues that start at five years old. I don't see a problem with that if the game is purely for fun: no emphasis on winning and everyone plays. It's also important if the child *wants to play.* My sister Peg asked me if her seven-year-old daughter should play traveling soccer. I said, "You're asking *me? Ask her.*" I think it's great if she really wants to play, which she did. My concern is for children who are forced to play. They'll inevitably lose the passion for the sport, and they'll burn out.

It's good for a young child to play a lot of different sports. I think specialization in any one sport begins way too early today. Children should sample all the sports they can while they're young.

Teaching sportsmanship is one of the great lessons you learn in competition. We don't harp on this a lot at Notre Dame, because sometimes I think we are too nice! We don't do a lot of trash talking. I really didn't learn sportsmanship as a player. I hated to lose and was never anxious to shake an opponents hand after a loss. I had the quickest handshake in the East! I've learned a lot since then, and a good coach should stress the importance of sportsmanship.

I like to read the comments of various coaches after a loss, and it's very interesting what they say. Often, when we beat a team, an opposing coach will talk about what they did wrong, without ever giving us any credit. Yet other coaches will credit the opposition, and that just sounds a whole lot better. I want to make sure I don't sound like a poor sport.

I want my players to be good sports, but I also want them to have confidence. This is a fine balance between having a little swagger and being a good sport. I don't want them to back down. I want them to go toe-to-toe, without being overbearing, cocky, and arrogant. If an opponent starts trash talking, they can talk back, but they better be able to back it up. I'd rather they let their playing do the talking.

It's a big step in a coach's evolution to not take player performance personally. If a team is performing poorly, the players are not doing this *to the coach*. If you think this way as a coach, it will create a division between the coaches and the players. It makes everyone think me versus you, rather than *us*. We are all in this together. It's not the coaches against the players, but it can so easily get to that point. A coach has to find a balance between demanding the best of the players and being understanding.

I think this is where our football coach, Tyrone Willingham, excels so well. He demands much of his players, and, yet, you don't see him picking on a player or blaming any one player in the press. That's balance. And it shows.

⑦ HANDLING FAILURE

If it wasn't for the dark days,
we wouldn't know what it is to walk in the light.

— EARL CAMPBELL

I'm convinced that we learn more from our failures than our successes. My first four years here were very good. We won 20 games each year. But my fifth year we had our first losing season. I had known nothing but success up to that point. That was tough. I remember the point in that season when it became mathematically impossible to finish with a winning record, and I didn't handle it well at all. It was also the year that my son, Murphy, was born, so I felt some stress that year. It was a very tough year and I remember my husband, Matt, saying, "You have to lighten up, it's not the end of the world and you're taking it out on us." I felt like my whole life was tied up in winning. It was all that mattered. After a loss, I wouldn't talk to anybody or I'd get emotional, or both. I even started thinking that I wasn't doing my job and that maybe I should resign before they fire me. I was, after all, hired to win.

Nothing was working that season. The team chemistry was bad. There were no bright spots. Every loss was the end of the world. I hated it. I just couldn't stand losing. Now here is the ultimate irony; we got into the NCAA Tournament! We got an automatic bid for winning the conference tournament. Our record was something like 12-14. So, of course, now I'm thinking, "Great . . . we're a trivia question now! The first losing team to ever go to an NCAA tournament!" We won three games at the end of the year to get there, so I thought maybe we'd keep playing well. Wrong. We went to UCLA in the first round and just got killed.

It was awful, and I was glad the season was over, but I learned a lot because I handled that season so poorly. I learned a lot about handling adversity. I learned that I was a role model and leader, and those kids were looking up to me. And yet I was falling apart. I let my whole life go bad because of this one basketball season. It forced me to do some introspection. I began to question what I really wanted, and how I could get it. How can I fix it? I decided to stay, obviously, and give myself a chance to turn it around. I had to accept the fact that we weren't that talented that year. They were nice girls, but they weren't the best on all the high school recruiting lists.

The chemistry was not there, mainly because I knew nothing about chemistry at that stage of my career. I just took five players, threw them out there, and said, "Let's play." I just lived basketball because that's how it was when I played. We never saw our coaches off the court; it was just all about basketball. Coaches taught, and then we all went home. The coaches weren't involved in our lives off the court. They couldn't tell you how I was doing in school, and probably didn't care. That's how I used to coach, especially that season.

I was a bottom-line coach. I'd look at stats and say to a player, "That's it, you're not playing well, we're losing, so I'm playing someone else." I never considered how it made that girl feel. I couldn't relate to bench players because I was always a starter. I didn't treat bench players like they were important. I just wanted to win. Winning was paramount, and my sole reason for coaching. That year was rough, and the next one was pretty shaky, too. One of our freshmen, Beth Morgan, came by for a visit. Beth is like me. I could yell and scream at Beth. I could say anything I wanted to her. She just wanted to win. She always knew what she did wrong before I yelled at her. She worked so hard and was such a great leader. But she was the exception. I had to learn a lot about how to treat people.

Reflecting on that season, I knew it was a disaster, but I also knew it was my fault. I decided then that I had to start showing some compassion, and that I had to get to know the players outside of basketball. I had to learn how to show that I cared about them not just as basketball players, but also as people. I didn't know how to do that because I'm not a nurturing, compassionate person by nature. I'm not the mom in the neighborhood who has all the kids in for milk and cookies. You don't have to be nurturing and compassionate to coach men, but you sure do to coach women. I even had a former player once tell me I should coach men. At the time, I thought it was a compliment. It wasn't.

Nobody likes criticism, and nobody likes failure. But you learn a lot from both. Sometimes you have to step back and reflect, but if you look closely, there are lessons to be learned from failure. After a loss, I was just terrible in practice. I'd really work them. And two days later, I was still mad. I was mad until our next win! And during that season, that was usually a long time! I used to carry it with me for so long that inevitably the team would lose its confidence, because clearly I had lost confidence in the team.

Today when we lose, I can figure out what went wrong and move on. But I do have to see the film and come up with a practice plan before I can put aside a loss. I'm not comfortable until that film is in my possession. I usually bring the film home. Sometimes I don't watch it right away, but I'll wake up at 4 A.M. and put the tape in.

That's what happened our championship year when we played at Rutgers and lost. We were 18-0 coming into that game, so it was our first loss all year. I have a lot of family out there, and my sister Patti came down after the game and brought a grade school team with her. We talked, took pictures, and my sister commented on how mature I was in handling that loss. I usually don't socialize after a loss. I either stay in the locker room until most people are gone or I hurry out of there as fast as I can. One year after a loss at Villanova, I even used my mother as a screen to get through the crowd and out to the bus!

It's a good thing my sister didn't see me later after that Rutgers game. My manager didn't tape the game, figuring since it was on TV we could just get a copy from the network. We flew home and I had no tape. I was livid. I was screaming at her. I have a friend in New Jersey who taped the game. I had my friend get that tape on the next available U.S. Air flight and spare no expense. It cost me about $150. Price was not an object. I told my assistant I was going home, and to meet that plane and get that tape to my house by 10:15 that night.

The men's team was playing at home that night, and on my way home, I realized what a jerk I was for throwing that tantrum. I got mad at myself over that one. That was the first game we lost all year, for crying out loud! So I turned around and decided to go to the men's game to support the team just to prove to myself that I can handle this, that I can rise above it. I stood in the tunnel at that game, clapped for about five minutes and then decided I couldn't handle it anymore and went home. But it was a step in the right direction.

Again, I was mad at myself after that Rutgers game. I always feel like a loss is my fault. At the end of the game we were down by one point with just less than 30 seconds to play. I told them what to run, but we had trouble breaking the press and didn't even get off a good shot. I should have called a time-out, but there is always something like that after every game. I can only think of one loss in my entire career where I didn't find something that I would have, or should have, done differently. It was in that same championship season that we lost to UConn in the Big East Conference Tournament finals when Sue Bird scored at the buzzer. When I walked off the court after that one, I thought that was a great basketball game. We played a great game, they played a great game, and they made a shot at the end. Even that game, if you consider it a failure for us, probably propelled us to the national championship. That Notre Dame team hated to lose, and losing right before the NCAA Tournament was good timing because I knew we would practice really well going into the tourney.

Sometimes failure doesn't look like failure on the outside, but to me it is when our team fails to reach its potential. We won 18 regular season games in 2002–03, but we underachieved. The thought of failing to reach one's potential can be haunting to live with every day during a season. You can't feel sorry for yourself or cry about it, because if you do, you'll lose confidence and play tentatively. You'll play worse. You have to get angry. You have to work harder.

The most devastating loss in my career was the loss to Texas Tech a few years ago in the NCAA tourney. The winner advanced to the Elite Eight. We were up 17-0 at one point. A few minutes later it was 17-17. How do you lose a lead like that? That one really hurt. Not only was that our last game of the season but the Final Four was also in my hometown, Philadelphia, and I really wanted to get there. That took me more than a year to get over. Two years prior we had beaten Texas Tech in the tourney on their home court, and they were the number one seed. So, I guess things even out. But that was a crushing loss. But even there, we learned. We regrouped and committed to turning it around. And one year later we won the national championship.

The loss isn't nearly as important as how you respond to it, and my teams tend to respond well. Of course, fear is a great motivator. We practice hard after a loss, hard enough that the team doesn't want to lose again. We've had some tough losses, some lopsided losses, in which it is very difficult to draw anything positive from them. One example is the loss two years ago to Tennessee in the NCAA tourney. We fell behind fast and that game got away from us. In fact, I thought we even had some players quit on us in that game. Sometimes I wonder if players intentionally foul themselves out of a game just to get out. That's not going to help you improve, but we'll use games like the Tennessee game as a motivator for the next game.

We'll use opponent comments as motivators, too. You always hear about "bulletin board material." Well, we have a bulletin board. We research what our opponents are saying about us and post it. Two years ago, prior to the Boston College game, we found some quotes from one of their players on the Internet. We posted that and played really well in beating them.

Nobody is successful all the time. If you were, you wouldn't be able to handle failure. Failure doesn't have to be the end of the world. It can be the beginning. Sometimes success is just around the corner, even though you might not know it at the time. I remember in 1997 we went down to Georgia Tech, and I recall our situation looking pretty grim at the time. We had lost some players for various reasons. Danielle Green and Niele Ivey, who was just a freshman, were finished with season-ending injuries. Diana Braendly had left the team for personal reasons. With only seven healthy players, no one was feeling very cheery about the rest of the season. It also happened to be Thanksgiving, and no one was feeling particularly thankful. We sat down to a private Thanksgiving dinner, and I asked Letitia Bowen to say grace. She prayed, "Lord, we don't understand why these things have happened to our team, but we know that you have a plan for us, a plan that we are not privileged to see, but a plan that we will follow. Amen."

And follow we did! We went on to win the tournament at Georgia Tech with Katrina Gaither scoring 40 points in the final game. We went on to the Final Four with seven healthy players, and a manager that we suited up. And four years later we won the national championship with a team that was led by fifth-year point guard Niele Ivey. Faith is tested during failure, and that faith can lead to success.

(8) HANDLING SUCCESS

The harder the conflict,
the more glorious the triumph.

—THOMAS PAINE

When I first arrived at Notre Dame, I wasn't thinking about a national championship. Not yet, anyway. I was thinking about getting into the top 20. I said in five years I wanted to be in the top 20. Four years later we did get in the top 25, but we didn't get in the tournament. We were ranked 18th—they only took 32 teams—but still we didn't get in. That's when I learned the importance of scheduling. We had a couple of losing seasons after that, and although no one likes to lose and I certainly don't wish a losing season on anyone, you learn a lot in those seasons. In fact, you probably learn more in losing seasons than in winning seasons. I learned, and I made a lot of changes.

A lot of ingredients go into building a national championship team. One of the biggest changes for us was joining the Big East Conference. Although I can't take any credit for joining the conference, we learned early that you have to play a pretty high level of competition in order to be successful. It doesn't do you any good to play 20 teams that you can beat and pad your record. Eventually, you'll play a tough game, and you'll probably lose. You'll probably lose badly, and you'll be exposed. Joining the conference catapulted us onto the national scene. It gave us instant credibility. We were always pretty good before joining the conference. We usually won 20 games, but we didn't play the right competition. Then we'd play someone in the top five, and we couldn't beat them. We almost had to go undefeated just to get noticed by the NCAA Selection Committee. What we learned was that the schedule was so important. You don't have to play the top five all the time, but you have to play and beat the teams that are ranked about 15 to 40. Scheduling is totally under our control. We choose it ourselves, and we choose it very, very wisely and carefully.

I share this scheduling philosophy with our players. I tell them the games in November and December are practice games. That's all they are. We are just trying to improve. Wins and losses don't matter. Our goal is to get better each game. Then we get to the Big East season and we need to be playing better. But even with conference play, the goal is still improvement. In fact, some games we would win, but I'd be disappointed because we still didn't play very well. On the other hand, some losses were okay if I could see improvement. The important thing is to play to your potential.

In the 2001–02 season, we lost an early game to Colorado State. They were ranked and they did have a great team. We played at their place, which is a tough place to play, and only lost by a few points. After the game I thought we played well. It was a great game, we did some good things, and I'm okay with that.

We are always playing for March. In March, we can play the worst game of the season, but as long as we win, I'm happy. We need to win enough games during the season to get into the tournament, but we need to be playing the best basketball we can by March. Then winning becomes everything, but we sure can't be worrying in March about a game we lost in November.

I say this only to a young team like the one we had a couple of years ago. I won't say this to a veteran team, because I want to raise the bar some. But two years ago, we played three ranked teams right off the bat and lost them all. We were 2-4 and then 6-5, and I thought we were in trouble. But while playing weak teams early might get you some wins, it also builds false confidence. You begin to think you're better than you are, then you play a ranked team and get annihilated and your confidence is shattered. I just kept hammering home the point that it doesn't matter. We need to win 18 games to get to the tournament. We just need 18 wins, and I thought we could do that.

Then we got to Big East play and wiped the slate clean. It's a new season, and we're 0-0 now. We started very well and got clicking a little bit, then Jackie Batteast got hurt and that set us back some. But we followed our plan. Our upperclassmen were a little unrealistic. They thought we would be right back in the Final Four again, but that was a fantasy when you consider that you need great leadership to be successful, and we didn't have it.

I used to predict our record; I'd get out a pencil, look at our schedule, and mark the games I thought we should win. Somewhere I must have had this great epiphany, because I just stopped doing it. What happens is that you work very hard to get ranked, and every Tuesday I would run to get the USA Today and the women's poll to see where we were. We'd get six votes, and then eight, and then we got in the top 20. Then it was like we were never again allowed to lose. We worked too hard to get here, and a loss would knock us out again. The pressure that I put on the team, and myself, was incredible. During the national championship season, I never looked at the rankings. Although when we got ranked number one that season, the increased media attention was hard to ignore, which in a way probably helped prepare us for the media circus at the Final Four. But even that ranking didn't affect the team.

In fact, that national championship team is what grounded me! For the team it was a four-year process, but for me it was a 14-year process. I'll admit that I was excited to be ranked number one. The day we got ranked, of course, they wanted to do a press conference. So I called Ruth, Niele, and Kelley to come over for the conference. I was pretty excited, and they were totally composed! They asked Ruth how it felt to be number one, and Ruth said that we expected to be there. They asked Kelley how it felt, and she thought they were referring to her broken hand and she said something about how it's healing but that she'll play in a makeshift glove. Niele said something about how being number one didn't feel much different today than yesterday. And I was in awe of them thinking that those were really good answers!

It was the same way during the NCAA Tournament. We were playing in the regional in Denver, and right after practice, word had spread that Xavier had just upset Tennessee. Before I could say anything, Kelley Siemon said, "Let's make sure that doesn't happen to us!"

The year after the championship, I told them "don't worry about the rankings because we won't be ranked." Then we got ranked and the freshmen went through that whole pressure thing. And the next game they played horribly, couldn't hit a shot, and they didn't even realize it. Suddenly you're ranked, and you play differently. You realize quickly that rankings don't matter, except in March. You have to experience it, I think, in order to deal with it.

It's the same thing with getting to the Final Four. The first time, no one really knows how to handle it. We were simply happy to be there. There was a sense that the program had arrived. Unfortunately, that's how I approached it. I told the players to go enjoy it. Take pictures! Have fun! We're going to dinners, and being interviewed on ESPN! We looked like tourists. And we lost. Afterward, I realized that I didn't approach it the right way. The last time we went, it was so different. It was all business. Without me having to say a word, the team knew—this was about winning. We were incredibly focused. We learned how to handle success.

I talked to my mentor, Jim Foster, who has been to the Final Four, about how to handle that, and he helped me out a lot. The media attention at the last Final Four was amazing. I was particularly worried about Ruth. She was going here and there for interviews, and to accept various awards, and I was concerned this would be a distraction to her game. Luckily, she was mature enough to handle it. It's good to get there because it raises the level of expectations to the point that getting there is no big deal anymore. It's simply expected. And no one wants to be the team that didn't go to the tourney for the first time in 10 years.

While upgrading our schedule was important to the program's success, the biggest thing that helped us, as a team, was when I began to focus more on defense. I used to try to outscore our opponents. Let's score 90 points! Then I did the statistics one year, a year or two before we made our first Final Four. I did stats for our wins and stats for our losses, and what I found was in our losses we were giving up about 80 points per game! In wins, we were giving up 55 to 60. Most of my practice time was devoted to offense because I love to tinker with offense. We started doing a lot more work on defense. We normally use a 2-3 zone, which isn't exactly brain surgery, but you have to do it well enough to make the other team take shots it doesn't want to take. You also have to be flexible enough to find a defense that suits your team. Some coaches will claim to be a man-to-man coach, and use nothing but man-to-man. That's all well and good, unless you don't have man-to-man type players. You have to adjust to what your team is and play to your team's strengths. The championship team wasn't deep, so we didn't press much, and we played a lot of zone. The current team has some depth, so we play a little more man-to-man, and maybe press a little more. Some coaches will say, "Don't get beat by your man." We work a lot on what we do when and if someone gets beat, the defensive rotation, because players—even great players—get beat. I don't think you can have six or seven defenses and be good at all of them. On the other hand, opponents will figure out how to beat your defense eventually, and you have to be able to go to something else. We kind of made the decision to stick to 2 or 3 defenses, especially with a young team, and to concentrate on playing them well.

Recruiting also became a huge part of our success. I've learned a lot about recruiting through the years. As I mentioned earlier, if I go to a girl's house, and that house is a shrine to that girl, I don't want to recruit her. I changed our recruiting philosophy. I hired Carol Owens. Then I recruited Beth Morgan. That was the beginning of the program's rise. Carol really upgraded our recruiting. She did a great job of identifying the players that would fit in here. Before that, we were all over the place recruiting. We had a lot of kids who couldn't take us to the next level. Some of them just didn't fit in well. We also didn't always get our top choice, and sometimes we'd end up with a class of "backups." I really didn't have a system in place. Carol changed all that. She had a great eye for talent, and the kids loved her. The parents loved her. We started to sell the idea to high school players that you can be the one to take Notre Dame to the next level. It was an idea that worked very well with Beth Morgan.

Beth and Katryna Gaither came in and that really got us rolling, because they were foundation-type players. We really hadn't had that before. Then we put some complementary role players around them, and we became a pretty good team, and a good program. They got us to the Final Four, which helped recruiting and, ultimately, landed the Ruth Riley class.

Getting Beth Morgan was a challenge. Stanford was after her, and Stanford had just won a national championship. Vanderbilt was after her, and so was Indiana. We told her she could go to Stanford, win another national championship, and be just another member of that team, or she could come to Notre Dame and be the one to lead us there for the first time ever. She's not a cocky kid at all, but she liked the challenge we presented. Katryna, on the other hand, was a sleeper. She wasn't highly recruited. Her dad said she was going to be an All-American. We thought, "yeah, we've never heard that from a dad before!" This dad was right.

I learned that you have to get kids who want to be in the program. Yes, I'll try to sell you on Notre Dame, but I'm not going to the point where I have to change your mind to get you to come here. I want the player to be the one who says, "Notre Dame is the place for me." Notre Dame is not the place for everyone, and I'd rather have 12 kids who really want to be here than 12 kids that I had to talk into coming. This means I may pass on a player who is ranked in the top 5 or 10 in the country if I don't think she'll fit in here. There are plenty of good players out there. If I get the 25th player, that's fine because I know she's good. Player rankings don't really concern me. Chemistry is most important. I want a player that I'm going to enjoy coaching, and one that the team is going to enjoy playing with.

I don't know which is harder, winning a national championship or repeating, but it took a long time to get a national championship. I'm anxious to repeat, but as John Wooden said, "I wish all my friends one national championship, and all my enemies two!" To be honest, I want to get back to the Final Four, but I wasn't expecting it the year after we won the championship. We had graduated three starters and five seniors who provided great leadership and talent. The year after the national championship we were ranked 15th in the preseason, and I thought that was a gift. Yet our fans and the media and everyone else thought we were getting no respect at all! Sure enough, we proved what a gift that was when we dropped out of the top 25 almost immediately, but, eventually, built our way back in.

Getting back to the Final Four is not easy, but there is one major difference now. *I know how to get there.* I have a map now that I didn't have before. I have a plan that I know works. I'd like to do it soon while we still have some players who have been there before, rather than have to do it with a whole new team.

The players on that championship team handled the success extremely well. Ruth Riley got almost all of the attention. We had five seniors, and Megan Leahy and Imani Dunbar were as much a part of that success as anyone else. These were two seniors who got no attention, no notoriety. Nothing. But they came to practice every day and tried to make Ruth and Niele better. That was their job, and they took great pride in it. Their attitudes were tremendous. They were happy for Ruth. Had they not accepted their roles, it would have hurt team chemistry, and we wouldn't have won. In every interview, I would always talk about those two, and try to talk less about

Ruth. I was hoping if the team would see that, they would accept and embrace the idea, too.

Ruth was always deflecting the attention and was very good at crediting her teammates for her success. She was amazing. Ruth could not escape the attention. Ever. She couldn't hide. She could wear sunglasses and a hat, but she's still six-foot-five. She had a really tough time with the attention initially, because Ruth is a very private person. She had people knocking on her door. Everywhere she went she was mobbed. We used to talk about it a lot. My husband protected me. He screened my phone calls at home, and I have an administrative assistant at the office, but Ruth had no one.

In truth, the players probably handled the success better than I did. The attention was too much. Suddenly, I was in a glass house. I'm a private person. I drive fast, but I never honk at anyone or yell at anyone for fear of the attention I would draw to myself. I remember when we were ranked number one, it would take me about 45 minutes to walk from the media room to my office because I was signing autographs. It completely overwhelmed me. I was totally unprepared for it. I didn't know it would ever get that big. We've always had great support from our fans, but this was unreal. For a while I wanted to stay home. My friends helped me get out of the house.

One year someone suggested I go out before games and greet our fans. At first I didn't want to. I'm way too nervous usually. Greeting fans helps take my mind off games, but at 20 minutes before tip off, I'm in the locker room, totally focused on the game. I don't like being the center of attention, so this was a big adjustment for me. I wish someone had called and warned me. I called Geno

Auriemma at UConn to find out how he handled all of the attention. Yet you can't complain because you would never trade it for the championship. You can sound unappreciative, but at the same time, I wanted my life back.

Getting ranked number one is another kind of success. It was intense because I didn't feel like we could ever lose again. It was great to be seeded number one in the tourney, but now there were no more upsets. We were the favorites in *every* game. We like to wear our green uniforms, but you had to be the lower seed in the brackets to wear green. We were upset that we couldn't wear our green!

I had trouble finding my life again. I wanted to stay at home with my family, and often couldn't. I didn't like it and had a very hard time dealing with the fact that I would be recognized just about everywhere. I remember telling Matt, "We gotta get out of here." The San Francisco Notre Dame Club invited us out for the weekend. They wanted me to speak. I thought this was great! Let's go! We got to the hotel and I suggested we go out for a walk on the wharf. We were no sooner out there and I heard "Coach McGraw!" Some man had recognized me. I was in a baseball hat, sunglasses, no makeup, and he recognized me! Now, I feel like I have to wear makeup to go to the supermarket! Another time, we went to the Jersey Shore, which is somewhere we go every year. I was walking along the beach with my sister-in-law and a girl ran by and said, "Great season, congratulations." Again, I wasn't wearing anything with Notre Dame on it, nothing to identify me, but people notice anyway.

I guess I finally accepted it. You wouldn't have believed this office after the national championship. We received candy, gifts, flowers, and notes. We had to hire a part-time secretary to write thank you notes for us. We were over-whelmed by the support. The kindness of people just amazes me.

So was it worth it? You bet. I'd do it all again because I really want this team to experience that. I want them to see just how much fun this can be. I don't worry about repeat-ing, but once you've been there it's hard to sit back and watch someone else achieve what you want. I hope we do, but there is so much luck involved, too. The year we won it, nobody got hurt. That's luck. The schedule was favor-able in many ways. Our tournament seeding was favorable.

However, right after that season I addressed my biggest worry: complacency. I had a couple of players who I thought were really going to have a problem with this, so I addressed it immediately. I told them that my biggest worry was that they were going to get complacent and be polishing their rings all summer. We have six freshmen coming in. They're going to take your spots. That came true. We had two players who thought they would be the next Ruth. They thought that by simply being in the pro-gram, they were entitled to a turn in the spotlight. They never worked on their game. The freshmen came in, took their spots, and it became a huge problem.

Some players have a sense of entitlement. They think that just because they've been in the program they've earned the right to play. Just because you start one year doesn't mean your job is secure the next. There is always someone coming in who wants your spot. You have to work hard enough to keep it.

My advice for coaches who win championships at any level is don't let it go to your head. Next year you're starting all over again, and everyone is after you. I look at how they treat our football coaches here and what they go through. I know I'm a losing season away from that happening to me. There is that nagging voice that says you might not get back there. It happened after the Rice game in the 2001–02 season. I was very emotional after that and thought, geez, we might not even make the NIT this year. At that point, I started playing the freshmen. Coaching is a job that everyone in America can read about and judge you on. You can read in the paper where we blew another game. Our failures are such a public thing.

Another piece of advice is don't try to do everything. I have to turn down some invitations to speak here and there or to appear here or there. You can't do everything, and you'll wear yourself down if you try. I didn't feel like there was a break between the national championship and the next season. It just sort of rode into a new season. Take a break, enjoy it, but don't let it go to your head. Teams will be really anxious to pay you back. The year after we won the championship, everywhere we went, if we got beat, you'd think they had just won the national title.

We lost at Arizona the following year and they stormed the floor! Stormed the floor! I was thinking to myself, "What are they so excited about? We're not that good!" It's a compliment, I suppose, but I used it to fire up our team. I told them, "See that? That's how they feel about beating us!"

Players need to continue to improve. Even if you are the champs, there is always room for improvement, and you need to improve before next season. In fact, you have to work even harder than you did to get there in the first place.

9 PUT THE TEAM FIRST

It's amazing how much we can accomplish,
when nobody cares who gets the credit.

—LEON BARMORE

The year before we won the national championship, we had a really good team. We went 27-5, but the team chemistry was terrible. I felt strongly that Ruth Riley, who was then a junior, should be the focal point of that team, and there were a couple of players who really fought it. A couple of players wanted the attention, the stardom that Ruth was getting. Pat Riley calls this "the disease of me." Riley discusses this as one of the stages of growth a team must go through.

I think that because we went through this stage, the chemistry was so much better the next season, and we won the national championship. Nobody wanted to go through it again, because it wasn't fun. I think players look to me to make it fun, despite the fact that it's not my job to make it fun. *You* choose your attitude, not me. I never promise anyone that it will be fun. When you come into the gym, *you* can make it positive or negative. *You* can say it's great to be here or it's not. It's all how you look at it. Life is 10 percent what happened to you and 90 percent how you react to it. We had players that year who chose to be negative. It's amazing how one person can really ruin a team, ruin a season, and totally undermine your efforts. It just takes one. Yet, strangely, it doesn't work in reverse. One positive person cannot make it a great experience by herself. But one negative person can sure ruin it. This was one awful season, and everyone knew it. We won that year, and we had the talent to get to the Final Four, but we didn't play as a team.

So we had a team meeting at the end of the season, and I made them watch the film of the last game against Texas Tech, who beat us in the regional. We really should have won, and I made them watch the whole game. That was one brutal meeting. I really let them have it. I was brutally honest and told each player what she didn't do right.

Ruth Riley said, "I'm sick of these meetings and I'm not going through this again next year." I think they were expecting a happy meeting in which we celebrated a great season. I think they were shell-shocked. They couldn't believe that I still wasn't over that loss. I was still really angry at the whole season because it wasn't any fun. We had a pretty good season, I suppose, by most measures, except it wasn't any fun. And that's the bottom line.

We had meetings all season about this. We had team meetings. We had meetings with individual players. And I hate meetings. I've discovered that this is a good measure of team chemistry, too. If you're having a lot of meetings, the chemistry is no good. The national championship season, I don't think we had any meetings.

But I learned. Now, if there is someone undermining the team, my first action is to try to fix it. Failing that, I dismiss her from the team. Here's another area where it really helps to have team leaders. Nobody could fix this in the locker room for me. I could fix it on the court, but not in the locker room. Then again, it's strange how things work out, because I'm not sure we would have won a national championship the following year if we hadn't gone through that horrible season. It united the team. It reenergized the players. It forced them to refocus. It made them take responsibility for their own attitudes. At the time, I certainly didn't see this as the birth of a national championship team, but in retrospect that's probably what it was. In fact, I didn't even think we were a national championship contender until we beat UConn at home in 2001. Earlier in the year we beat Georgia, and I knew *they* were good. That's probably the first time I admitted to myself that we were really good. I thought we might be Final Four material, but when we beat UConn, I thought "we're not just good, we might be the best!"

Team goals have to be set realistically. After the national title season, some of my returning players actually thought we would be back in the Final Four the next year. That was hard for me to understand, because they are usually not that confident. And most of them didn't do the work that summer necessary to return to a Final Four, anyway. That made it tough because we brought in six freshmen, who felt the bar was raised and they had to get back to the Final Four. It must be our fault if we don't get there, they thought, because the team was there last year. And we really didn't have the team leadership to help them deal with the expectations.

I was more reasonable with the expectations. I told them our goals were to get into the NCAA tourney. I wanted to finish in the top four in the Big East because the top four get a bye in the postseason conference tourney. In my heart, I thought we should have finished second, but I never told them that. I wanted to host an NCAA first and second round game, but to do that we had to be a fourth seed or higher. We never set a specific win-loss record as a goal. Never.

We started the season 2-4, then 6-5, and I really started to wonder if we would make the tournament. It was really hard to balance the expectations of those few returning players who thought we should win it all and the freshmen, who weren't sure where we should be. It's different for a coach, because no coach goes in and says our goal for this year is to be right in the middle of the pack, even though that might be realistic. But I want the players to know I have confidence in them. So I really had to think about how to set our goals.

The Big East season gave us a new slate, a new season, and we started playing well. We needed leadership to tell everyone that we needed to overachieve that year. We asked players in practice, "Do you want go to the NIT? That's where we're playing right now! Or do you want to go to the NCAA?" So we used the goal to motivate. The freshmen knew we took some graduation hits. Clearly, you don't lose three senior starters including the national player of the year and not feel it. But the freshmen thought the upperclassmen would lead them, and they would just have to chip in a little bit.

All in all, it worked. I was happy with where that team finished, because I really feel that if Jackie Batteast hadn't gotten hurt, we would have made the Sweet Sixteen. With Jackie we would have done better in the Big East tournament, which means we would have won more games, we would have finished stronger, and we would have gotten a better seed. We still would have gone on the road, but we got a seven seed, and I think we could've been about a five seed. We certainly wouldn't have had to play Tennessee in Knoxville. We went from 6-5 early in the season to finishing with 20 wins. That's progress.

What about that Tennessee game? We needed a perfect game to play with Tennessee, and they had to play poorly. Neither of those things happened. I remember when the bid came out, there was dead silence in the room. The freshmen looked at me for a clue as to how to respond (Yippee, we're going to Knoxville!). We all knew how tough that would be, and it was. But is this team better for having gone through having to play Tennessee at Knoxville? Without a doubt. Eventually, I'm going to pull that film out. I haven't even watched it, which is a personal first for me. But I am going to pull that out eventually, and we're all going to watch it.

While sports take tremendous dedication, I do worry about player burnout. Every now and then, they need to get away from basketball because it is a year-round commitment. Every fall break, I give them time to go home.

I think freshmen need this especially. I worry about this because I don't know of many coaches who will give a team six days off that time of year. I'm never sure what we'll have when they come back. I also give them four or five days off after the Big East Tournament hoping they'll come back refreshed. I guess I'm a big believer in time off. Even our practice schedule, we try to go four days on, and one day off. I try to get them a day off on the weekend, and I'll even try sometime during the season to give them an entire weekend off. Players would rather not practice, of course. They just want to play games. Two weeks to prepare for a game sounds like an eternity for them, while I'm wishing we had *more* than two weeks to get ready. The season is a marathon, not a sprint, and you have to plan accordingly.

Players—even the most successful players—have to accept criticism. I have found this to be especially difficult for female athletes. Women tend to take it personally. They are very sensitive, and this current team is particularly sensitive. There are times when the coaches agree that whatever this player does today, it's great, and we're going to smother her with positive reinforcement. When I yell at a player, the head goes down right away. And I don't even feel like I'm yelling. I usually have two or three players on a team who I feel I can yell at. With everyone else, I have to be careful.

It's not uncommon at all to have tears in our huddle. It's just frustration from kids who want to, above all else, be good. It's not easy to build someone's confidence while telling her when she's doing something wrong. I think as a coaching staff we are generally very positive, and yet, if you ask the players, they probably wish we were more positive. I tell them, "When you play well, you'll hear the positive."

Strangely, even with the championship team, I knew I couldn't yell at them. They simply didn't respond to it. It didn't make them any better. In fact, that team had more to do with changing my coaching style than any other. I don't know if they responded to a more positive style of coaching, or if they were so good that they didn't make a lot of mistakes and I didn't have to critique them. Don't get me wrong. I explode. Sometimes I can't control myself. But I try to temper it. And, afterward, I always make sure the offending player is okay, and it's different for each one. Personally, I prefer players who I can yell at. It's easier, and I probably develop a better relationship in the end with them.

⑩ RECRUITING

All great achievements require time.

—DAVID JOSEPH SCHWARTZ

There are certain parts of recruiting I like and some parts I don't like. I like watching the best high school players in the country play against each other. I like going to their high school games. I like getting to know the players and their families. And that's where the enjoyment ends.

We begin recruiting at the age-14-and-under AAU tournament. These are kids who will be rising sophomores. The assistant coaches will go to the national AAU tournament for 14 and under, which is usually in July, and they'll try to see as many games as they can. We really don't concentrate on any specific geographic region. We recruit all over the country. I usually don't go to these tournaments, and I'm not sure how many head coaches do. But my assistants will go, and our recruiting coordinator will, too. Most top programs have a recruiting coordinator who doubles as an assistant coach. That's where recruiting begins. You get on our list because one of my assistants put you there.

So once the list is created, we try to go see them play a high school game during their junior year. This is where I'll try to get involved. I'll go out and see the top athletes play, but I really don't go to very many high school games. I'm lucky if I get to six or seven per year, because my focus obviously is on our current team. I would never miss practice or a game, so I try to find an off day when I can go, and I just don't have many of those. Carol Owens, on the other hand, will go to a lot more games than I. Then we start writing to players in their junior year, and we also go through their transcripts and make sure they can clear Notre Dame academically. We can start writing them September 1 of their junior year. We probably write weekly to those we consider our top prospects.

After our season that same year, we look at our list again and usually narrow it to about 10 prospects we are really going to target. We go see them play in April, and then we get one phone call in June to see if they are interested in us. Along the way, hopefully, they've been responding to us, so we have a pretty good idea of their level of interest in playing at Notre Dame. They've either been writing or e-mailing us. Maybe they've come to a game or two, or attended our camp. We'll try to get them to come onto campus unofficially in June. Most of the top players by this stage don't attend basketball camps. They play in top tournaments, like the Adidas tourney, but they don't do the collegiate camps anymore. Younger players usually attend camps. It's not until after their junior year that it really gets serious, at least from our perspective. It gets intense. Phone calls start. We're trying to limit our list, and they're trying to limit theirs. There really are no recruiting "seasons" because it is a year-round process that starts much earlier than most people realize. And this is why you need a recruiting coordinator. Once practice starts at Notre Dame, I'm totally focused on the team, and we need someone else to coordinate this, especially during the season.

The worst part of recruiting is the uncertainty. This becomes most intense in August. We get our list down; the players get their lists down. We could be in every athlete's final three, and yet not get a single player. There is no law of averages here. It's stressful, it's irrational, and there are no guarantees. It really becomes a crapshoot, and often we're held hostage to the whims of 18-year-olds. I want the best players, but I also want kids *who want to be at Notre Dame*.

One player who really wanted to come to Notre Dame was Megan Duffy. When we go to a recruit's house for an in-home visit, it's not unusual for the prospect to place balloons along the route every so often so that we can find her house. Megan marked a path for us to her house with signs every so often that read "Welcome National Champs."

It's not my job to go out there and try to talk some 18-year-old into coming to Notre Dame. We have a lot to offer at Notre Dame, and if a young person cannot see that, then maybe Notre Dame is not right for her. I get to a point where I stop trying to convince a prospect what to do, and let her make a choice. The problem is there are a lot of other coaches trying to convince her that their school is the right one. My approach is so laid back, I wonder if players misinterpret that I'm not as interested as some of these coaches who are more aggressive. But that's not my style. I will not beg. These young women are pulled in a lot of different directions, and there's a lot of pressure on them. It's a big decision for them and, for many, the first really big decision they've ever had to make. They need help and they need guidance from parents and coaches. Some parents say it's totally her decision, which I think is a big mistake. You can't tell her where to go, but you know your daughter, and you can guide her to make the best decision for her.

At the end of this whole process, I just want her decision. Yes or no. I just want to know. Being in limbo is the hard part. You really have no idea. Everyone is always asking me, "So how's recruiting going?" I always answer, "I have no idea. We're in with the players we want to be in with, but whether they come, I don't know."

The parents are very influential in the decision, more so than the high school coaches. Some high school coaches aren't very involved at all. And we try to find out who is the most influential and talk to them, but we really don't get a sense from the prospects which way they are leaning. In fact, I find out more about how a recruit is leaning by talking to other people, rather than the player herself. Ones that call you back, you can conclude, are probably more interested than those who don't.

Players choose schools for various reasons. Sometimes it comes down to choosing a school because she already has a friend playing at that school and they want to play together. Sometimes two players will meet at camp, become good friends, and decide they want to play somewhere together. Sometimes they'd rather stay close to home. Sometimes they'd rather go away. And it's different with every single young person.

Offering a scholarship can be extremely flattering for a teenager, sometimes too flattering, especially for the parents. It can be an ego trip for the entire family. I don't like recruiting players who enjoy the process. We used to have backup players that we knew wanted to come to Notre Dame, players that weren't on our A-list. The problem with that strategy is that you can end up with a team full of backups, and that's not good for the program. We don't feel like we have to do that here anymore. So we usually whittle it down to a list of 10 players. Then our strategy is first come, first served. We take whomever commits first. We tell them all that we want them to come, but if someone else on the list commits first, we're taking her.

To be honest, there are times when you have a great player and you say, "We got to wait for this one." We were going to wait for Jackie Batteast to make a decision. Even if she made us go all the way until March, we were going to wait for Jackie! She's a local player who we really wanted, but the fact is, that is rare. We recruit for specific positions and we try to get at least three prospects for each position. There may be one we like more than the other two, but the difference between the three athletically is just not that great. We are not going real far down our list. In other words, we would be happy with any of the three. The scary part of all of this is what if all 10 players reject

Notre Dame? In that case we could decide not to offer any scholarships, but that has never happened here. Some years we only need one or two players, which affords us the luxury of being more selective. We currently have a talented sophomore and junior class, and sometimes that's an obstacle in recruiting because of the depth chart and potential lack of playing time. But, more often, I find good players want to play with other good players. They have enough confidence to believe they can play with, if not overtake, the upperclassmen. I don't think many of them want to be the one player who has to carry the load, because they had to do that in high school.

Coaches and parents send us letters and videotapes of their players all the time. High school coaches have a responsibility to find college scholarships for their players. It's not a problem if you have a great player because everyone knows about her. It's that next tier, just under the radar, in which a coach may have to sell the player to a college coach a little more. You need to get a player seen. You need to get them in AAU. Most people think we see them during their high school seasons, but it's actually during the summer at AAU that you're most likely to get noticed. Make tapes and send them out.

In a year, we probably get between 300 and 400 letters, and about 70–80 videotapes. I don't know what other schools do, but we look at every single videotape. It's very time consuming, but we usually do that in April and May. If someone stands out on tape, we try to go to see her play in the summer. It is very rare that this process will lead ultimately to a scholarship offer, but even though the odds are against you, this is another way players try to make our list.

Generally, we know whom we're going to recruit, and odds are it's not going to be someone who wrote to us first. It's easy to identify your targets at this level, because everyone puts out a top 50 list, or a top 100, or whatever. *USA Today* puts out the top 10. There are recruiting services everywhere today, so there really aren't many sleepers anymore. It used to be you could go somewhere and find someone that not many people had heard about. That's not true anymore.

You also have to accept as a coach that you're going to lose some prospects you really wanted. We've lost a lot of players that we really wanted. One of them was Lisa Leslie. We had Lisa Leslie visit Notre Dame. She was down to three schools and we were one of them. I remember sitting in her living room thinking, "Boy, if we get her, we'd be set!" We offered her a chance to come to Notre Dame, but she ended up staying close to home and attended USC. That one hurt. But, she was very close to her mom, USC had a great program, and that's that. Unfortunately, there are more stories about big ones that got away than the ones you actually land. You do everything you can possibly do, which we did with Lisa, and then hope for the best. But you are going to lose great players, and Lisa was obviously a great one to lose.

We also got into Chamique Holdsclaw's final seven, but when she cut her list of schools down to three, we didn't make the cut. Rebecca Lobo was another one we really wanted, and she wanted to go to a Catholic school. I thought we had her. She really liked Notre Dame, Holy Cross, and Connecticut. But we signed Michelle Marciniak in the same year, and we lost Rebecca. That's how unpredictable recruiting can be. We really thought we could get Rebecca. She was Catholic, and she liked Notre Dame. That one hurt, too.

Fortunately, there are success stories, too. We are elated when we get that great player who we know can take us to the next level. We felt that way with Ruth Riley, Alicia Ratay, and Jackie Batteast. We really felt that way with Beth Morgan. That was huge. Beth was the cornerstone of our entire program. She's from Bloomington, her dad's the baseball coach at Indiana University, and we thought she was probably headed to IU. She was also considering Stanford, Vanderbilt, Virginia, and Notre Dame. I understand the Stanford coach went into Beth's home and laid a ticket on the table for Beth to visit Stanford. We went through weeks and weeks and weeks with her. We went to visit her for the home visit in September and discovered a great family. The family was very down to earth. Her dad, as a coach, understood the whole process. Then we heard she might visit Stanford, so we got in the car and drove four hours down to Bloomington just to chat with her for 15 minutes between classes at her high school! We were trying to do whatever we could at that point. We got in the car and drove four hours back. When she finally said yes, we felt like we really turned the corner.

We've had players who were top athletes that didn't pan out because we had to talk them into coming here. Who doesn't want to come to Notre Dame? At least that's how I think, but our program has obstacles to overcome, just like any other program, and those obstacles change constantly. When I first came here, the first obstacle to overcome was the perception that Notre Dame was just a football school. People thought no one cared about basketball here. Then we were fortunate enough to start winning and people saw the support we got from our administration, and they really don't say that anymore.

The next obstacle was the whole Catholic issue. Some folks thought you had to be Catholic to go to Notre Dame. I think I only have two Catholics on my entire team right now. Then there was concern over taking religion classes, and the myth that we were going to convert them. I actually had one mother say she was afraid her daughter might marry a Catholic boy!

Weather can be an obstacle. We recruit a lot against Duke and Stanford, and they got us beat there, compared to South Bend weather. Distance is also an issue, especially with girls. Most of them want their parents to see them play. We like to recruit the East Coast, but the East in the last few years has not been overly talented. I'm always asking Carol Owens, "Aren't there any great players in the Midwest?" Now, there are. But, geographically, I think girls like to be within five to six hours from home.

Academics play a part, too. Even if they can get in, they don't want the academic challenge of getting a degree from Notre Dame, not when they can go to a lot of other top 25 programs and not have to work as hard.

You hear a lot these days about negative recruiting, other coaches bad-mouthing Notre Dame. I think it probably happens even though we don't hear much about it, because recruits don't say anything about it. If I had a daughter who was being recruited, I would listen to each coach and then tell him or her, "Here's what other coaches are saying about you and your program. How do you respond to that?" You have to do that because coaches will say all kinds of things and appear authoritative, but they might be totally inaccurate. I would ask questions to get at the truth. Players and their parents don't question coaches during the recruiting process nearly as much as they should.

One example of inaccurate, if not negative, recruiting was the first year we went to the Final Four. We lost five players to injuries that season. Two of them were season-ending injuries. The word in recruiting circles the next year was that we ran five players off the team! Well, they were on the bench, they just weren't suited up. Then we heard how we were a flash in the pan. Morgan and Gaither graduated and we would never be good again. Coaches will promise kids they can get them into the WNBA, that they can get them jobs at ESPN, whatever. And prospects believe that stuff!

Poor game attendance used to be an issue here, but we've taken care of that, too. We've overcome the facilities. Our locker room used to be so bad we didn't even show it to recruits. We used to tell them it was closed for cleaning! College athletes today live in locker rooms. Today's locker rooms are elaborate. They have computers and televisions. Then we started thinking that if a recruit is going to base a decision on the locker room, maybe that's not the kind of player we want at Notre Dame. But, then again, two years ago we got a brand new locker room and, I hate to admit, it has become a recruiting tool. Players like it, and they don't mind hanging out there.

Sometimes, I go into a home and know immediately that recruiting this athlete was a huge mistake. Recently,

Carol and I made an in-home visit on a Saturday afternoon. We pulled up, rang the doorbell and the dad invited us in. We were looking around the living room and wondering, "Where's the girl? Where's the mom?" Neither one of them was there! The dad told us his daughter was still sleeping, and the mom had just run out to the store to get a few things! It was *their* idea for us to come at that time! I was ready to walk out that door, and I probably should have. Well, about a half hour later, the girl came down the stairs. The whole time I was thinking if she has no respect for me now, how is this going to work at Notre Dame? I really wanted to get up and leave, but I couldn't really do that. That same player came for a campus visit and made some comments to one of our players about how I liked another recruit better than she. That was another turn-off. She ended up going to another school, and that was fine with me.

So what impresses me on a home visit? I expect a prospect to look nice. She should be in appropriate attire, dressed neatly. I want her to make eye contact with me. I want her to ask questions. That shows interest. I want her to be assertive enough so that her parents don't do all of the talking. And, of course, she should hide her trophies!

I really get a good picture of the kind of person I'm recruiting when I get to see her interact with her mom and dad. I'm interested in how much she respects her parents. I want to know whether or not she's spoiled. I can learn a lot about how a recruit will be on our team just by looking at that relationship she has with her parents. I don't think the parents should be waiting on the daughter all the time. I remember being in a home once when the doorbell rang and the daughter said, "Mom, are you going to get that?" And I was thinking, "Geez, you're 18 years old, get off your butt and answer the door!"

Here's one thing I always notice when a player and her parents visit us: When they're on campus, they always go to the bookstore to buy a souvenir, and I notice which ones ask, even demand, a credit card from their parents. A recruit who says, "Thanks so much, Dad, for the sweat-shirt" or "No thanks, Mom, I really don't need a sweatshirt" impresses me. It shows how much she appreciates what she has and shows what kind of person she is. These are just some little things I pay attention to that are cues into what kind of people they are, and cues I'm sure they have no idea I'm noticing.

In terms of basketball skills, I look for intensity. I also look at how they play defense. Young players rest on defense. I like players with pride. I look at a recruit's face after someone scores on her. I hope it bothers her, because I guarantee it will bother *me*.

We look at ball handling and aggressiveness. Does she dive on the floor for loose balls? How is her defense? Here's where you can see intensity, or lack of intensity. It's not dif-ficult to be intense on offense, because everyone wants to score. But whom can she defend? Whom can she stop? Can she guard someone? Does she crash for rebounds, or just sort of hang around the outside? Does she sprint the floor every possession? Is she willing to take a charge? This is something that tells me she is a team player, she's aggres-sive, and she'll sacrifice her body for the team. This is the most unselfish act in the game of basketball. At any sum-mer game, if a player takes a charge, you'll see all the coaches in attendance take out a pen and make a note of it. A lot of great players don't want to take a charge because "it's not their job."

We look very closely at attitude. What happens when the coach yells at her? Is she making eye contact? Is she sulking? Is she pouting? When a player gets in foul trouble, is she complaining to the referees? How is she when the team is losing? Is she yelling at her teammates?

Actually, I prefer to see a recruit's team lose. When a team wins by 20, that's easy. There's no adversity. I like to see a player get into foul trouble. How does she handle the frustration? Does she possess self-discipline? I've noticed that with girls you have to see them play a lot to get a feel for them. They can be up and down. You can see a player on a great day, and on a bad day. The difference is striking. It can be the difference between offering her a scholarship and wondering why she was on my list in the first place.

In addition to skill level and attitude, we look at potential. Some players peak in their junior or senior year in high school. We want to see improvement from freshman to senior year. Players who peak as seniors generally are players who are fundamentally sound, but not particularly athletic. They're just not going to get a lot better. We look for athletes that have potential, particularly with post players because we have a great post coach here who really can turn a good player into a great one.

With guards we look at decisions. What kind of decisions does she make? This is also something very difficult to teach. You can teach a player how to pass, but you can't teach her when and where to pass. You can't teach her how to make a decision. You can get better at this by playing more, but not that much better. If a point guard is turning the ball over four or five times in high school, she's probably going to turn it over in college even more. We also want a player who is unselfish, but not unselfish to a fault. I want someone who's talking to her teammates, encouraging them. Who's talking in the huddle? I want a leader, someone who's in charge. I want someone who, when things go bad, is the one clapping the loudest. I want someone who says, "Give me the ball, I can beat this kid who's guarding me." We want someone willing to be that positive voice.

This may surprise some people, but I don't look at a lot of statistics. When I do, I look at percentages rather than actual numbers. A player can average 27 points in high school, but it could be because she takes 30 shots. I look at free throw percentage a lot. That's how I determine good shooters. A player who is shooting 50 to 60 percent from the line is not a good shooter. Period. The same is true with assists and turnovers. In fact, if there is a statistic that I am particularly interested in, it is assist-to-turnover ratio. If you have a good assist-to-turnover ratio, you are going to help the team. Rebounds are a good indicator, too, because you really can't pad your stats here.

I observe their overall communication patterns with teammates. I watch free throw huddles. I watch what happens when the team is losing. Who's positive? I watch their demeanor on the court. When they come out of a game, do they cheer for their teammates, or are they just waiting to get back in the game? I want leaders. These are really character issues more than basketball skills. Then of course, there are the God-given abilities—speed and size. It's true that you can't coach speed, and tall players don't shrink.

This may sound strange, but I was never a big fan of the really big center. I always liked speed. I wanted players who could run. Then Carol Owens saw Ruth Riley and said this is a player we have to have. I went to see Ruth play and really liked her, but that was unusual for me. I remember before Ruth, Kara Walters was at UConn, and she always beat us, but I didn't care. I still didn't want a player like that. She was big, but not a running-type player. Then I saw Ruth play, and I started to change my thinking a little bit. And Carol is a great post player coach. Having had Ruth, of course, I now want a player every year like Ruth! A player like that can change the entire face of a game, both offensively and defensively. It's great to have someone who can score consistently around the block. Players today don't want to do this. There are just not many true centers out there. Even in the WNBA, there are very few players who enjoy getting physical in the post, trying to post up and score down low. Most players want to shoot threes, handle the ball, run the point, or do all three. I want to score 90 points per game, but, of course, I always want to hold our opponents to 50. I like to run, but I'm also big on shot selection. In fact, if there is one thing I'm known for, it's shot selection. I'm really particular on who takes what shots. Not everyone has the green light to shoot threes.

I'd like to see some changes in the recruiting rules. One that just changed recently for men, but not for women, is our level of participation at AAU games. All of these college coaches attend the women's games, and then afterward we all line up to talk to the coach. It's a little like visiting the Pope, although you don't have to kiss the coach's ring. It used to be we would have to write notes for the coaches to pass on to the players. Thank goodness they stopped that one. So you stand in line for no other reason than to say hello and let the coach know you were at the game. There has to be a better way. The men's coaches resolved this with no contact, period. They can't talk to the coach or the player, not even if you see them in the hotel lobby. I don't mind talking to AAU coaches and, in fact, I've learned a lot from them. I just don't like standing in line to do it. And you have to do it, otherwise you appear, at best, disinterested or, at worst, absent.

I also don't believe prospects need five official campus visits. Three is plenty, and every recruit should be able to get down to three finalists. There should also be a limit, in my opinion, on in-home visits. Some prospects will line up a dozen home visits, yet you only get five campus visits! Some recruits enjoy the process a little too much. A lot of times the parents enjoy the process too much, way more than the player! The parents are often saying things like "keep an open mind" or "you have to be fair to everybody" even though their child has a pretty good idea of which schools interest her.

This is how recruiting really is. Don't trust what's reported in the media or on the Internet. A lot of times I'll see reports that I'm recruiting someone. Well, it depends on your definition of "recruiting someone." I'm sending out hundreds of letters, but I'm certainly not "recruiting" hundreds of players. And players are getting letters from *everyone*. It doesn't mean they're getting scholarship offers.

They may not even hear from that school again. For anyone who wants to know when the recruitment turns serious, it turns serious when the coaches attend your high school game. You can get a lot of letters from the same school. It still doesn't mean anything. Every school is going to narrow its list down, but when a coach attends your high school game, you've made the short list.

Young athletes need to ask better questions during the recruiting process. The one question players don't ask is the most obvious one: Are you offering me a scholarship? It amazes me that they never ask that! As I said, we tell them first come, first served. Other schools are slow playing an athlete as a backup, in case another player doesn't commit. They may try to schedule a campus visit for November, hoping they get an early commit in September from someone else, and, therefore, never have to go through with the November visit. Players need to ask about that, but they don't. They need to ask, "How long will you wait for me?"

A player should also know that a school's interest is serious and genuine when she begins to receive personal, hand-written notes from the head coach. If the head coach comes to see you play in your junior year, you're in pretty good shape, though this is not always true. Sometimes I'll see a prospect's name on a lot of lists, so I'll put her on my list, too. Then I see her play, and she's just not what I'm looking for. But, generally, if the coach is there, it's a good sign.

Players who want to get noticed by Notre Dame should respond to the letters I send out and contact me for an unofficial visit if they want to come to Notre Dame.

She should come to our camps and let me know she wants to come to Notre Dame so I can be sure to watch her play. We've had that happen. Jeneka Joyce came to our camp her sophomore year in high school. Sheila McMillan came to our camp in eighth grade. Jill Krause came to our camp in seventh and eighth grade. Send the tape, send the letter, and come in person. That just might get you on the list.

⑪ PERSPECTIVE

*Don't let making a living prevent you from
making a life.*

—JOHN WOODEN

My son, Murphy, has given me a new perspective and even more so now that he has started playing sports. Now I sit in the stands watching as a parent, and I see the coach talking to my son. The light bulb goes off in my head as to how I've yelled at some of my players, and I wouldn't want my son treated like that. Basketball was such a big part of my life, but he has taken such a big part of it now. In 1997, we were on the bus going to play at Texas in the second round of the NCAA tournament. Murphy was sitting with me on the bus. I was a nervous wreck. We had never advanced in the tournament before, and now we had to win at Texas in front of

10,000 screaming Longhorn fans. He reached over and patted me on the leg as if to say, "We're going to be okay, Mom." I'll never forget that moment because I realized this is just a game, and he's my *life*. Immediately it removed the stress and tension. It reminded me what was important.

Sometimes it's easy to forget that basketball is just a game. It's easy to get caught up in the moment, in the wins and losses, in the national championships. Then something happens to remind you just how trivial basketball really is. Thank goodness we have these little reminders in life to keep our priorities in order, and there was no bigger reminder for me than September 11.

It was the summer of 2001, and we were recruiting—specifically, we were putting our home visits together for September. We were only going to make four home visits. We were recruiting Nicole Wolff, who lived in Boston. We were also recruiting Courtney LaVere, who eventually did commit to us. Courtney was living in Los Angeles. We went to see Megan Duffy on September 9 in Ohio, and from there we went to Boston to visit Nicole. After the visit with Nicole in Boston, Assistant Coach Kevin McGuff was going to come back to Notre Dame, and I was going to meet Carol Owens in Los Angeles.

Basically we were making our own flight arrangements and I had checked with Anthony Travel and knew there were two direct flights on September 11 from Boston to Los Angeles, on either American or United Airlines. I really wanted to take a direct flight to Los Angeles, where Kevin's flight departed from Providence with a stop in Detroit to catch another flight on to South Bend. I told Kevin there was no reason for me to go with him, because I really didn't want to stop in Detroit, even if he had to. Kevin, on the other hand, was not too excited about driving me back to Boston to catch my direct flight. He was willing to do it, but he also let me know it would be quite an inconvenience and preferred we leave together from Providence. I relented and agreed to fly with him out of Providence, through Detroit, even though I knew it would take me forever to get to Los Angeles. I called the travel agency and told them to forget the Boston to Los Angeles plan and that I would fly out of Providence with Kevin instead.

We were sitting on the plane in Providence the morning of September 11 when the pilot came on the intercom and said, "We're under a little bit of a delay right now." The flight was supposed to leave at 9:45 A.M. A few minutes later, the pilot came on and said the radar had been shut down across the country, that all planes have been grounded and we're all going to get off the plane, go back into the airport and find out what's going on. But they really didn't tell us anything. We got into the airport and gathered around the televisions like everybody else, and got there just in time to see the second plane hit the World Trade Center. My husband, Matt, called me on my cell phone, and I still didn't know what was going on. He asked me where I was. I said, "Providence." Matt thought I was on the doomed plane, because last he knew I was going from Boston to Los Angeles. When he told me that was the flight that hit the World Trade Center, I just burst into tears and sobbed hysterically. I couldn't even talk. I told Matt, "I'm only in Providence because Kevin didn't want to drive me to Boston!" Thank God Kevin didn't want to drive to Boston. If I had been by myself instead of with Kevin, I would have been on that plane.

So we were walking around the airport and we ran into Mike Brey, who was also in Providence. We rented a car and drove home 15 hours to South Bend. It really hit me, because I really wanted to be on that plane, and easily could've been. I remember thinking the whole time that I just wanted to be home with Matt and Murph. For a long time, I didn't want to go anywhere, and I just didn't want to travel. I wanted to stay home. Nothing seemed important except staying home. I cancelled the rest of the recruiting trip.

We eventually had to go out to Denver and we did, even though Matt and Murph didn't want me to go. And I didn't want to go. Matt and Murph didn't want me flying, and to this day Murph doesn't want me to fly. Murph didn't know all of this happened until someone said something to him at school. We talked about driving to Denver, but we ended up flying. I wasn't afraid to get on a plane; I just didn't want to leave home. We never did go to California and visit Courtney.

I didn't want to talk about this to the media at the time because it was very personal for me, and way overblown. It probably started when Matt said something to someone and the next thing I know it's on ESPN and totally blown out of proportion. The stories were that I was in Boston and stepped off the plane at the last minute and all that. I wasn't in Boston, and I wasn't even ticketed for that flight. But that was my original plan, and the whole thing was very emotional for me. I heard from people I hadn't heard from for years. I still get chills, and I guess I felt more blessed than lucky. I felt like someone was watching out for me, and in this case I think it might have been Kevin McGuff.

Suddenly, basketball seemed trivial. Remember, in the end, basketball is just a game. And like all games, it's supposed to be fun.

ABOUT MUFFET MCGRAW

To understand the competitive fire that has fueled much of McGraw's success, you have to go back to her playing days. A four-year starter at Saint Joseph's University in Philadelphia, Pennsylvania, she captained the 1976–77 Hawk team which finished 23-5 and was ranked third nationally. In four seasons, McGraw helped her team compile a 59-12 mark, while participating in the regional Eastern Association for Intercollegiate Athletics for Women (EAIAW) once and the national AIAW tournament once.

She received her bachelor's degree in sociology from SJU in 1977. Following graduation, she coached for two seasons at Philadelphia's Archbishop Carroll High School where she guided her teams to a 50-3 record, including a 28-0 mark during her second year. That season, she led her squad to the Catholic League championship and was named coach of the year for the Philadelphia Catholic League.

McGraw then played point guard for one year with the California Dreams, a team in the since-folded Women's Professional Basketball League (WBL). She returned to her alma mater in 1980, serving as an assistant coach for two seasons under Jim Foster.

In 1982, McGraw was named head coach at Lehigh University, leading that school to unprecedented success. Her teams were 88-41 (.683) during her five-year tenure. She was named East Coast Conference Coach of the Year following her first season with the Engineers in 1982–83. Her '84–85 and '85–86 teams posted back-to-back 20-win seasons, finishing 20-8 and 24-4, respectively. The latter squad won the most games in women's basketball history at the school, while claiming both the ECC regular-season and tournament titles.

Hired at Notre Dame on May 18, 1987, McGraw's penchant for success made her a logical choice for the position. In 16 seasons at Notre Dame, Coach McGraw has led the Fighting Irish to fourteen 20-win campaigns (including a current string of 10 straight), 10 NCAA tournament appearances (including a current streak of eight straight), five Sweet Sixteen berths, two trips to the Final Four, and the 2001 NCAA title. To put those numbers in perspective, Notre Dame is one of only six programs in the country to have posted 10 consecutive 20-win seasons, while the Irish are one of just eight teams in the nation to advance to the NCAA Sweet Sixteen five times in the last seven years. When combined, McGraw is one of only five coaches in America who can boast two current streaks of that caliber. She has posted a 363-138 (.725) record during her tenure at Notre Dame and owns a career mark of 451-179 (.716) in 20 seasons as a collegiate head coach. The architect of Notre Dame's rise to prominence, McGraw has shown no signs of slowing down any time soon. In July 2002, the veteran head coach signed a five-year contract extension, which will keep her patrolling the Irish sidelines through the 2008–09 campaign.

Success for McGraw has meant coaching great players. Ruth Riley, the 2001 Big East Player of the Year, became the third Notre Dame player to earn AP All-America honors when she was named in 1999 to the third team. Riley, who was a unanimous first-team all–Big East selection in 2000 and was the 1999 Big East Defensive Player of the Year, also earned Kodak honorable mention All-America honors. She also was a member of the 1999 USA World University Games team and a finalist for the 2002 USA World Championship team.

Besides Riley, two players whose names are forever linked to elevating the Notre Dame program to national prominence are 1997 graduates Beth Morgan and Katryna Gaither. The two-time Kodak and AP honorable mention All-Americans both scored more than 2,000 points during their careers, becoming the first two players from the same team in NCAA history (male or female) to reach that milestone. They rank one and two, respectively, in career scoring, while Gaither also stands as the school's second all-time leading rebounder behind Riley. Both players went on to careers at the professional level with the now-defunct American Basketball League (ABL) and the Women's National Basketball Association (WNBA).

The trio of Riley, Morgan, and Gaither highlight an impressive list of 17 Irish players who have garnered all-conference honors during McGraw's career. In addition,

the Notre Dame mentor has coached two conference
players-of-the-year, three league rookies-of-the-year, and
11 conference all-rookie team selections since arriving in
South Bend.

Thanks to McGraw's ability to always get the best out
of her players, Notre Dame has developed a solid presence
in the WNBA in recent years. Coquese Washington, a 1992
graduate and current Irish assistant coach, is a point guard
for the Indiana Fever. In the 2001 WNBA draft, three starters
from Notre Dame's national championship squad—Ruth
Riley, Niele Ivey, and Kelley Siemon—were chosen. Riley
was the fifth pick overall by the Miami Sol, and when the
Sol was folded last year, she was the number one overall
pick in the 2003 WNBA dispersal draft by the Detroit
Shock; Ivey was a second-round pick of the Indiana Fever
and has been a mainstay in Indianapolis the past three seasons; and Siemon was drafted in the third round by the
Los Angeles Sparks. In 2002, a fourth starter from that
title-winning team was drafted into the WNBA, when the
Detroit Shock chose Ericka Haney in the third round.

McGraw's knack for developing talent also extends to
the coaching ranks. No less than 14 of her former players
and/or assistant coaches currently are serving as coaches
at either the high school or college level. In addition, five
of her former pupils are presently collegiate head coaches:
Sandy Botham, a 1988 Notre Dame graduate who is at
Wisconsin–Milwaukee; Beth (Morgan) Cunningham, the
leading scorer in Irish history from 1993 to 1997 and now
the skipper at Virginia Commonwealth; Liz Feeley, a former Irish assistant now at Smith College; Bill Fennelly,
another former aide who is piloting Iowa State; and Kevin

McGuff, a Notre Dame assistant for six seasons before accepting the top spot at Xavier in June 2002.

In addition to her accomplishments on the court, McGraw has been a master recruiter for Notre Dame women's basketball. The Irish coach and her staff have attracted top-20 recruiting classes in each of the last seven seasons, including the 2001–02 freshman corps, which was rated third in the nation by Blue Star Basketball. Only two other schools in the nation have had seven straight top-20 recruiting classes, a testament to McGraw's abilities and the respect she has garnered from coaches, parents, and players around the country.

McGraw also has worked closely with Notre Dame administrators on promotions to increase interest and attendance in Irish women's basketball. Since 1999, season ticket sales have jumped more than 700 percent and the crowds at Notre Dame home games have reflected that surge. The Irish have ranked in the top 10 nationally in attendance in each of the last three seasons, highlighted by a school-record average of 7,825 fans per game in 2001–02, good for eighth in the country. In fact, all of top 20 crowds in school history have come on McGraw's watch, with 19 of those gatherings occurring in the last four seasons. Leading the way are Notre Dame's first two women's basketball sellouts—January 15, 2001, versus top-ranked Connecticut, and February 24, 2001, for Senior Night versus Georgetown.

On a national level, McGraw has been widely regarded as a champion for student-athletes. In June 2002, she accepted an invitation from U.S. Secretary of Education Rod Paige to join the new Commission on Opportunity in

Athletics. Created 30 years after the passage of the Title IX antidiscrimination law, the 15-member blue-ribbon panel examined ways to strengthen enforcement and expand opportunities that will ensure fairness for all college athletes. McGraw was the only women's basketball coach on the commission, which also featured former WNBA great Cynthia Cooper, U.S. National Soccer Team captain Julie Foudy, and two-time Olympic gold medal swimmer Donna DeVarona.

On top of her tireless work at Notre Dame, McGraw often is in demand as a featured speaker at various camps, luncheons, and other fundraisers around the country. Besides basketball, she recently has begun cultivating a passion for golf, sporting a 16-handicap. In fact, one of her favorite moments off the hardwood came just two months after winning the 2001 national championship, when she stepped to the fourth tee at Notre Dame's Warren Golf Course and promptly drained her first-ever hole-in-one.

Born December 5, 1955, in Pottsville, Pennsylvania, McGraw was inducted into the Philadelphia Big Five Women's Hall of Fame in 1989 and the St. Joseph's Athletic Hall of Fame in 2002. In 1997, she was named an honorary alumna by the Notre Dame Alumni Association and received an honorary monogram from the Notre Dame National Monogram Club. She and her husband, Matt, reside in Granger with their 13-year-old son, Murphy, born April 29, 1990.

MCGRAW'S COACHING RECORD

Year	School	Record	Pct.	Honors
1982–83	Lehigh	14-9	.609	East Coast Conference Coach of the Year
1983–84	Lehigh	13-9	.591	
1984–85	Lehigh	20-8	.714	
1985–86	Lehigh	24-4	.857	East Coast Conference Champions
1986–87	Lehigh	17-11	.607	
5–year Lehigh total		**88-41**	**.683**	
1987–88	ND	20-8	.714	North Star Coach of the Year
1988–89	ND	21-11	.656	MCC Regular Season and Tournament Champions, NWIT Tournament
1989–90	ND	23-6	.793	MCC Regular Season and Tournament Champions
1990–91	ND	23-9	.719	MCC Regular Season and Tournament Champions, NWIT Tournament, MCC Coach of the Year
1991–92	ND	14-17	.451	MCC Tournament Champions, NCAA First Round
1992–93	ND	15-12	.556	

Year	School	Record	Pct.	Honors
1993–94	ND	22-7	.786	MCC Regular Season and Tournament Champions, NCAA First Round
1994–95	ND	21-10	.677	MCC Regular Season Champions, NWIT Tournament
1995–96	ND	23-8	.742	NCAA Second Round, WBCA District II Coach of the Year
1996–97	ND	31-7	.816	NCAA Final Four, East Regional Champions
1997–98	ND	22-10	.688	NCAA Sweet Sixteen
1998–99	ND	26-5	.839	NCAA Second Round
1999–2000	ND	27-5	.844	NCAA Sweet Sixteen
2000–01	ND	34-2	.945	NCAA National Champions, BIG EAST Regular–Season Co–Champions, AP Coach of the Year, Naismith Coach of the Year, WBCA National Coach of the Year, WBCA District I Coach of the Year, BIG EAST Coach of the Year
2001–02	ND	20-10	.667	NCAA Second Round
2002–03	ND	21-11	.656	NCAA Sweet Sixteen

16–year Notre Dame total 363-138 (.725)
9 NCAA Tournaments, 12 Postseason Appearances

21–year career total 451-179 (.716)